Other titles in the Norfolk Origins series:
1: Hunters to First Farmers (published 1981)
2: Roads and tracks (published 1983)

Text © Poppyland Publishing, North Walsham 1987
Drawings © Sue White 1987
ISBN: 0 946148 24 4
Published by Poppyland Publishing, North Walsham, Norfolk 1987
Designed and Printed by Speedprint Design, Spalding, Lincolnshire
Typeset by PTPS Norwich
Printed in Great Britain.

Warning
Reference to or representation of a site, track or road should not be taken as
evidence that such a site, track or road can be seen or may be visited. In many
cases sites are on private land. Not all Roman roads are rights of way.

3: CELTIC FIRE & ROMAN RULE

By Bruce Robinson and Tony Gregory
in collaboration with the Norfolk Museums Service

Map: Tony Gregory

Illustrations: Susan White

Aerial Photographs:
Norfolk Archaeological Unit - Derek A. Edwards
University of Cambridge Committee for Aerial Photography
Suffolk County Council Planning Department

The aerial photograph that drew archaeological attention to the Icenian site at Fison Way, Thetford. The dark cropmarks represent the three ditches which surround the enclosure, while the surrounding mackerel pattern is geological. What looked like a simple site from the air proved very different when it was excavated.

(Photo: Suffolk County Council Planning Department.)

Front Cover: A reconstruction of the fort at Brancaster - see page 83.

Contents

Introduction

This third publication in the Origins series follows the pattern of its predecessors in a sense that it carries the story of Norfolk forward.

"Hunters to First Farmers", our first title, told of that vast period of time, over half a million years, stretching from the stone techniques of Palaeolithic man through to the arrival of a knowledge of the use of iron. The second, "Roads and Tracks", emphasised the influence and importance of lines of communication and recounted the story of Norfolk's pre-Roman and Roman tracks and roads and the county's subsequent planned road systems.

Thus it may seem strange that this publication, the most substantial so far, actually covers the shortest period of time, from about 500 BC through to the breakdown of Roman rule in this country circa AD 410. A span of less than a thousand years.

But what years! This same period saw not only considerable technical advance but also one of the most complex and eventful moments in Norfolk's long history.

It is one of the most exciting to study, too. For the first time in that long history it is possible to perceive tribes and places which can be identified and people who can be named.

In essence it was a thousand years which contributed enormously to the Norfolk we know today.

THE IRON AGE

Landscape of Norfolk

Norfolk had been farmed for some 3500 years before a knowledge of the use of iron reached these shores, so a pattern of cleared landscape - a mixture of arable and pasture - and tracts of thick, almost primeval forest had already emerged.

In general the boulder clay was too heavy to plough. Thus the central core of Norfolk, roughly, from Dereham to Attleborough and as far south as Diss, was still largely covered by virgin forest. Some was previously cleared land which had subsequently regenerated.

What are now the Halvergate marshes were then tidal mudflats, while Flegg and Lothingland were islands in the waters of a wide delta fed by the rivers Bure, Yare and Waveney. It was a vast expanse of water and creek.

To the west of the county the coastline stretched roughly from Wisbech to Downham Market. North of this line the fens were a wet and impassable chain of lagoons.

At the northern end of the chalk ridge, in the Docking area, the quality of soil was deteriorating. High chalk areas cleared in the Neolithic and Bronze periods had been over-exploited and too heavily farmed. Now the soil on the upper slopes was being washed away. Arable activity was diminishing, or had stopped, though some areas were still being used for pasture.

The climate was slightly warmer than might be expected today, and the sea level higher by about a metre. This meant that the uncontrolled rivers, wandering across their flood plains, undoubtedly caused serious flooding each winter. Indeed, most of Norfolk's present well drained valleys would have had numerous watercourses or at least one major stream.

This helps to explain why many Iron Age sites are found on the slopes rather than at the bottom of the valleys. It also suggests that communications were difficult and that communities tended to be isolated.

Agriculture

Settlements on the slopes used the wet valleys as grazing meadows in summer. The sides of the valleys were ploughed probably by farmers using simple wooden ploughs pulled by oxen. Higher land, particularly in

7

the chalk and the Brecks, was of little use for arable farming, so sheep and cattle tended to predominate. In the central forest block, it was pigs.

Villages seem to have comprised groups of farmsteads growing early forms of corn including emmer and spelt (varieties of wheat) and increasingly, barley. Indeed, beer seems to start here. Brewing was such a complicated and time-consuming business that the drink must have been an important element in Iron Age life.

No large settlement has been excavated in East Anglia. Friable pottery, degradable building materials, metal corrosion and centuries of farming activity mean many sites have simply been ploughed away. However, there is evidence that settlements were probably the size of modern farmyards, perhaps surrounded by a ditch and fence, and embraced two or three circular houses with mud and timber walls and thatched roofs.

The houses were warmed by a central fire, but there was no hole in the roof. In fact the heat and smoke caused moss and lichen to grow inside the thatch and act as an extra waterproofing agent.

In the farmyards were cylindrical pits for the storage of winter grain. Between six and 10 feet deep, they were covered by lids of plaited basketwork smeared with clay. The damp was an advantage. Damp germinated the grain closest to the sides, producing carbon dioxide which then flooded the rest of the pit to prevent the remainder of the grain from germinating.

A fair proportion of stock was over-wintered on hay, grain and fair weather grazing. The surplus was killed and the meat smoked, salted or dried. Iron implements were beginning to be introduced, too. In general, the cultivated areas of Norfolk created a landscape of small fields, ditches, hedges and tracks.

The people of the Iron Age were careful scavengers. There was very little waste. Most broken, worn or obsolete artefacts were taken apart or used for something else.

It was subsistence level living, but this does not necessarily imply deprivation or poverty. It means they provided for themselves, rather as subsequent North American frontier settlements were, of necessity, independent.

In the basics of life Norfolk was largely self sufficient.

Iron working

Iron had been in general use in central Europe for 300 years before it reached Norfolk in about 650 BC. Bronze was retained for a time, but iron became the predominant material. Locally, some low grade ores were available, the Greensand deposits of west Norfolk being the most important. Other materials were traded either in the form of prepared metal or finished items.

There were two concentrations of iron working settlements, one around Middleton and including Blackborough End and Setchey, and the other in the Snettisham area. Specialist smiths did much of the work.

Iron was a crucial new element, of course, and in order to obtain the implements and benefits a surplus of goods and produce was needed, as in the Bronze Age. Now, however, the range of artefacts was far wider and much more important.

It could not be melted or cast. These were future techniques. Instead, nodules of iron ore from the Greensand region were packed into clay furnaces with layers of charcoal. Bellows took the fires up to temperatures of about 800 degrees Centigrade. The impurities melted and ran out, leaving behind a spongy mass of iron and slag. This was placed on a charcoal smithing hearth and hammered to extract more slag. The iron then absorbed carbon from the charcoal, and the result was a low grade carbon steel.

First and foremost the smiths made weapons, mainly swords and spearheads; and then agricultural knives, billhooks, sickles, scythes and spade tips. Much of it was unadorned because iron is difficult to decorate. Iron also provided a more effective cutting edge than either flint or bronze, so its gradual adoption increased the efficiency of farming and land clearance.

The Iceni

The inhabitants of Norfolk in the Iron Age belonged to a group which the Greeks and Romans referred to as Celts or Gauls. These tribes were spread across Europe from Czechoslovakia to Britain, and seem to have spoken languages similar to those which now survive in the modern "Celtic" languages of Ireland, Scotland, Wales, Cornwall and Britanny. The exact moment at which the Iceni emerged as a discernible tribe is not known. There are no surviving records.

This lack of knowledge runs deep, for as a single tribe the Iceni cannot be perceived at all until a mere 50 years or so before the Roman conquest. Indeed, archaeologists still have to rely almost solely on Roman historians and administrators for the names of most of the British tribes. The one and only tribal name to appear on coinage of the period, happily, is that of the Iceni.

From these two sources - coinage, and written record - the name of the tribe at the time of the Boudiccan revolt is indicated.

Further evidence can be found in the name of the first administrative centre founded by the Romans at what is now Caistor St Edmund and which was then called Venta Icenorum. It is believed that Venta was a Celtic word for market place. So Venta Icenorum, in all probability, meant "market place of the Iceni."

Even so, many questions remain. There is no certainty that the Romans, for the sake of adminstrative ease, did not amalgamate a number of local tribes under the single name of Iceni. For example, eleven tribes surrendered to Caesar when he landed on British soil in 54 BC, but none of the names listed by the Roman historians are recorded again with the single possible exception of the Ceni Magni. There is no proof that the Ceni Magni were the Iceni, but the single word "Ecen" on some coinage suggests this is at least a possibility. If so, it is another indication that the word Iceni might be a slightly inaccurate Romanised attempt to tidy up the records.

Echoes of the word may also survive in Icknield, the Neolithic trackway - "the road leading to their land" - Ickworth and Icklingham. Though the origin of Icknield is not known it may be derived from Iceni. On the other hand Icknield might be a generic name for Medieval tracks.

North of the river Nar the generally accepted line of the Icknield Way appears to have little connection with the distribution of Iron Age finds. This has led to speculation that the accepted route, on some maps, is actually a post-Roman distortion perhaps caused by the Saxon town of Thetford, and that the Way's pre-Roman course might have been further west along the fen edge. The idea does present a number of problems, among them the matter of crossing rivers, a particularly difficult task in winter.

In the event large numbers of coins from Norfolk and Suffolk bearing the name "Ecen" and evidently dating from AD 43 to circa AD 61 seem to be evidence of a unified tribe. Find spots also suggest the Iceni were spread across Norfolk, Suffolk (down to Southwold and Bury St Edmunds), and on an island in the middle of the fens where March and Stonea now stand.

In contrast, relatively few coins have been found in the afforested middle section of the county, so the main centres of the Iceni may have been dispersed. Coin concentrations suggest at least four general locations - Norwich and Caistor St Edmund, King's Lynn and Snettisham, Thetford and Bury St Edmunds, and the fen island.

However, it is difficult to be precise about the nature of Iron Age tribes. The actual picture which emerges is of a constantly shifting framework which may have been stabilised into a formal structure by the Romans.

Tribal structure

Celtic society was cleft by deep and strict divisions of class. We know this from accounts left by Julius Caesar, who wrote about Celtic Britain and France circa 50 BC, and from later Irish sagas which encapsulated a great deal of information remembered from earlier Iron Age days.

At the apex of society was the king, whose power was a complex combination of political, religious and military influences. He was leader of the tribe's warriors and they, particularly the young men, were bound to him by personal loyalty. In return he fed and housed them until such time as they married and set up house on their own.

As religious leader the king was also supported by a priestly class which Caesar called vates, or bards. Other Greek and Roman authors used a word which is more familiar - Druids.

However, it is as well to forget the theatrical nonsense perpetrated at Stonehenge by well-meaning romantics every summer solstice. Actually, very little is known about the religious beliefs and ceremonies of the Druids or of Iron Age society in general.

According to Caesar, however, Druid ceremonies were held not in buildings but in wild places by the sides of rivers, at springs, and in clearings in the oak forests. Wells seem to have had some sort of special significance, too, because when disused they were often filled by unusual groups of objects such as pots, animal skeletons, and beds of hazel twigs.

It is possible these wells were of great importance when in use, and when out of use had to be filled in a particular way. This may be the origin of the Derbyshire custom of well dressing which is practised today.

The role of the Druids was wider in scale than mere involvement in religious ceremony, however. They were also teachers, astronomers, and the keepers of records in written form and as long, detailed epic poems which retold the history of the tribe and were passed from one generation to another.

So these were the most important classes - king, warrior, Druid. Below them, of course, was the great mass of the tribe, the majority, the peasant farmers who actually produced the food and the means to support those higher in the social scale.

Known living sites in Norfolk are few and far between, but this does not mean the population was small. Indeed, a balance of evidence suggests there were tens of thousands of Iceni tribesmen working the land and producing the wealth which distinguished this part of England.

Iceni coinage

Coins were in use in Britain from about 100 BC. Most of the earliest were of gold, and a majority were simple copies of the gold staters of Macedonia, a currency universally accepted throughout the Celtic and the rest of the known world. As the century wore on, however, a number

Four Icenian silver and one gold (far right) coins. All show a horse on the reverse (tails) side: the obverse (head side) pattern varies.

of Celtic tribes began to issue their own identifiable coins for local use. These often carried distinctive patterns and the names of individuals who may have been the chiefs or kings.

For some reason the Iceni seem to have been a little late in getting in on the act. When their coins did finally begin to appear about 10 BC these, in turn, copied the coinage of the Catuvellauni and Trinovantes of the Home Counties and Essex, tribes which were among the earliest to be identified in this way.

The early Iceni coins were also made of gold, but silver was quickly introduced. All of them had a sprightly horse on the reverse (tails) side. The obverse (heads) of the silver coins carried one of three distinctive patterns - a ferocious looking beast sometimes identified as a boar, a roughly sketched head with hair like porcupine quills, or a pair of back-to-back crescents.

It is not clear what the three designs represented, but it is possible they related to inter-tribal divisions such as favourite religious cults or even sporting or social groupings.

Almost half of the coins had a name inscribed beneath the horse. These were often the name of an individual, of which the most common was "Anted", which may have been short for Antedios, or something similar.

At the same time by far the most common inscription was "Ece" or "Ecen", which may have been the Celtic name for the tribe. If this is the case then the Romans may have recorded it wrongly as Iceni instead of Eceni. In any event this is the only example in Iron Age Britain of a tribal name, rather than a individual's name, appearing on coins.

One interpretation is that the Iceni were originally ruled by kings (in which case Antedios was in charge circa AD30) and that later a different system was employed. Something like a republic, for example. This could explain why the tribal name became more important than the name of a single individual.

The torc trade

Indications of the wealth of Iron Age Norfolk come to us mainly in the form of gold.

From the Latin word meaning "twisted", torcs were heavy rings of precious metal, sometimes gold, sometimes silver, but more often an alloy of the two called electrum. They were made from bars, or wires, twisted together into cable configuration which was then completed with decorated terminals.

A conclusion is that they were probably worn around the neck as a symbol of wealth and power, or perhaps placed round the neck of a statue in a tribal shrine in order to display the wealth and prosperity of the community.

The most famous torc discovered so far was found at Snettisham in north west Norfolk in 1954. In fact this particular corner of the county has produced more than a hundred torcs and fragments of torcs in the last 50 years. Many were buried as part of caches of scrap metal - unlike the great gold torc - and most were battered and bent and ready to be melted down to be made into new pieces of jewellery.

It seems possible there was a flourishing tradition of precious metal working in the area north of King's Lynn in the first century BC. Gold and silver smiths seem to have produced large numbers of torcs, probably to special orders, and to have exported them over much of Britain. The furthest discovery so far was made at Netherurd in the north of Scotland.

So many torcs have been found over the years in the "torc field" at Snettisham it seems likely there was a workshop nearby. Indeed, it is probably more than a coincidence that 700 or 800 years earlier, in the late Bronze Age, there was also a flourishing metalworking tradition in the same Snettisham area. This part of the county may have been a metalworking centre of very long standing.

Decorated end of the great electrum torc from Snettisham.

Decorated terminals of torcs from Sedgeford (left) and North Creake (right). Note how similar the patterns are to each other and to those on the Snettisham torc, surely all products of the same bronzesmith or workshop.

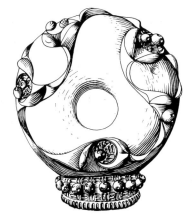

In any event the quality of workmanship in the torcs is of the highest possible standard. Snettisham's craftsmen must have been very highly regarded, for nowhere else in Britain has such fine material been found.

It is interesting to note that if coins are disregarded then the greatest proportion of this country's Iron Age gold and silver has come to light in Norfolk. This might mean Norfolk was particularly rich. Or there could be another explanation. Outside the territory of the Iceni a majority of Iron Age coins were made of gold. Silver was relatively rare. Among the Iceni, however, silver coins were more common than gold. Therefore, and for reasons unknown, it is possible the Iceni kept most of their gold invested in torcs while the rest of the country melted its gold down to make coins.

If so, it is an example of Norfolk sticking to old fashioned ways.

Bronze working and horse gear

Naturally enough it is the gold and silver which attracts most of the attention today, but it should be remembered these same craftsmen also produced fine work in other metals.

In a hoard of bronze objects from Ringstead, only a few miles from Snettisham, was a pair of bridle bits decorated with exactly the same style of ornamentation as some of the torcs from Snettisham. If the same man did not produce the torcs and the bridle bits then they were surely produced in the same workshop.

By this time, of course, bronze had been replaced by iron as a main metal for tools and weapons; but bronze was commonly used for making items of decoration. It was easily available, cheaper than iron, and a particularly easy metal to work.

Viewed in museums today bronze objects are usually green. When new they would have been a bright burnished red-gold colour. It seems to have appealed particularly to the Celtic sense of display.

Some of the bronze was used for personal decoration. For the ladies of the Iceni, for example, there were small and rather plain brooches. Most, however, was saved for the men and particularly for the warriors who insisted on looking their best for battle. While their swords and spearheads were made of iron the scabbards which contained the swords, and the warriors' helmets and shields, were often of bronze. These were richly decorated with flowing Celtic patterns, sometimes engraved into the metal and sometimes inlaid in red, blue and yellow enamel.

A lot of bronze was also used to decorate the chariot in which the warrior was driven into battle. The ponies' bridle bits, terret rings, hooks to hold the traces, plaques to cover the junction of the harness straps, and knobs on the end of handholds, would all have been made of bronze, and richly decorated.

The actual amount of wealth put into a chariot and into a warrior's equipment was enormous. It is an indication of how important the warriors were in tribal society.

Of course, although we know of the products of the craftsmen of north west Norfolk we know nothing of the men themselves. Or even if they were men. In contrast to all this it appears that some of the iron working was carried out separately not by specialist smiths but by individual farmers producing what they needed for themselves. This suggests the bronze smiths and precious metal workers were highly regarded. They may have ranked higher in society than the peasants.

An Iron Age warrior and his charioteer. Also illustrated are a number of bronze items associated with horses, including some from the Ringstead finds.

Kingdom of the horse

The horse seems to have induced a very special feeling among the people of the Iceni. It is the one repeating motif on coinage, and it is clear a great deal of wealth was spent on their well-being and decoration.

These were not the great chargers of medieval knights or the destriers (hunting horses) of medieval barons; but animals the size of stocky mountain ponies standing about 12 hands high.

There is no actual evidence that Iron Age horses were ridden or that they were ever used to pull farm vehicles. It is even possible that the later arrival of Roman cavalry provide the Iceni with a first glimpse of horses being ridden. If so, then the saving of them for warfare meant they were considered to be very special indeed.

It is interesting that the only survival of the name of the tribe, apart from placenames, is the adjective "ickeny" which was used in the dialect of Norfolk and Lincolnshire for things awkward and difficult to manage, and particularly for difficult horses. Could this have been a memory of the Iceni as horse dealers and breeders?

Earthwork forts

Throughout most of Britain the best preserved remains of the Iron Age are the hundreds of hill forts which cover areas such as the chalk downs remains of a Norman castle built a thousand years later the Icenian fort. Both the Iron Age and the later Norman fortifications acted as strongholds of Wessex. Some of these were actually towns, with dozens or even hundreds of houses tucked safely inside the banks and defences of deep ditches and high ramparts, often two or three deep. This defence in depth was needed because many warriors were skilled in the use of slings.

It is somewhat surprising there are so few of this type of fort in East Anglia. Where they do exist the shortage of hills meant they were often built on low ground overlooking river valleys.

The best preserved Iron Age earthworks in Norfolk are Warham Camp, near Wells and Thetford castle, in south west Norfolk.

At Warham a pair of ramparts and ditches enclose a circular area which could have been big enough for a population of 500 to 1000 people. Alas, there has been insufficient excavation inside the rampart to test the theory.

Thetford castle is more spectacular, with ramparts more than 20 ft high. However, only a third of the circuit survives. Inside the castle there stands a great motte almost 100 ft high. This is the remains of a Norman

The Iron Age fort of Warham Camp, near the north coast of Norfolk. The site was originally a perfect circle, surrounded by a pair of defensive ramparts and ditches, but landscaping in the 18th century removed the defences down one side, and the River Stiffkey now runs where they formerly stood. The pale stripes in and around the fort are the results of modern hay-making.

(Photo: Derek A. Edwards, Norfolk Archaeological Unit, 1976.)

castle built a thousand years later the Icenian fort. Both the Iron Age and the later Norman fortifications acted as strongholds guarding the important river Thet crossing of the Icknield Way where Nuns' Bridges now stand.

Three other forts in Norfolk may date to the Iron Age, those at Holkham, Narborough and South Creake. None of these has been accurately dated and none are as spectacular or as well preserved as Warham Camp or Thetford castle.

In the absence of excavations inside the forts it is not known if they had the same function as hill forts in other parts of the country. It is possible, however, they were small defended towns which would have acted as places of refuge for the surrounding countryside if danger threatened.

In some ways it is odd they are all ranged along the western portion of Norfolk. It is possible the Iceni in the rest of the county lacked defended sites altogether. On the other hand they may have been destroyed over the last 2000 years.

Trade

From about 50 BC onwards traders from the Roman empire and particularly from France began to carry on a widespread and presumably lucrative trade with the tribes of Britain. The main points of entry were on the south coast near Poole in Dorset, and Essex and the Thames Estuary.

Classical historians record that the tribes imported mainly luxury items and exported corn, hides, slaves and hunting dogs. It is possible a slave trade in Britain was created by the local kings specially to supply the Roman market.

Incoming luxury goods were no doubt intended for the top echelons of the social order, while exported goods were either the materials the peasants produced, or the peasants themselves.

However, the classical writers do not mention one item which archaeology tells us was imported in great quantity: wine, in large pottery containers known as amphorae. It may have been a desire for wine which persuaded British tribes to participate in the trade in the first place.

Amphorae have been found in Essex and the Home Counties, on settlement sites and in burials, but they have not so far appeared within the territory of the Iceni before the conquest. For some reason the Iceni seem to have been excluded from this interchange with the empire.

Some sort of economic isolation is further underlined by evidence from coinage. Although coins of the Catuvellauni and the Trinovantes are found scattered widely over southern England, they seem to have penetrated the kingdom of the Iceni only rarely. Again, Iceni coins are hardly ever found outside of the homeland.

It may never be known if the isolation was political or purely economic, or both.

No evidence has yet come to light in Norfolk of an Iron Age iron furnace. This is a Romano British iron furnace, based on the remains of a furnace excavated at Scole. The furnace man is using wet clay to plug a gap which has appeared at the bottom close to the nozzle into which the bellows fit. Techniques in the earlier centuries were probably very similar.

THE ROMANS

Early incursions

Roman troops first appeared off the coast of Britain in 55 BC when Julius Caesar, engaged in the conquest of Gaul, also decided to lead a major scouting expedition to these islands. The project was short lived, however, and fraught with difficulty.

The following year he returned with a better equipped fleet and an even larger army. This time they were successful. A bridgehead was established on the Kent coast and the local opposition beaten off. Then, in a deliberate display of Roman might, he marched his troops to London, probably little more than a small community at a crossing point on the river Thames.

Once this physical barrier was overcome, again in the face of armed opposition, Caesar prepared for battle with the most important of the tribal groupings, the Catuvellauni, under king Cassivellaunus. The decisive confrontation took place at the tribe's own fortified capital near modern St Albans, which was stormed and captured by the Romans.

Oddly, Caesar made no move to extend his influence. He seems to have decided he had done enough. Instead, he fixed the rate of tribute (tax) to be paid annually to the empire, and returned to Gaul.

On the face of it the incursion of 54 BC was pointless and seems to have achieved little, but it may have had at least one important aim, to dissuade the British tribes from lending assistance to their Gaulish cousins across the Channel. Caesar was already facing armies made up of Gaulish warriors and British mercenaries. So his two expeditions may have been designed to impress upon the tribes the awesome power of the Roman military machine.

There was one other important result. The Trinovantes of Essex, enemies and neighbours of the Catuvellauni, had called on Rome for assistance in their struggle. It may have worked; but within 50 years the Trinovantes were taken over entirely by the Catuvellauni who built themselves a new capital at the old centre of the Trinovantes at Colchester.

Within a few years, too, Roman traders began to penetrate Trinovantian territory along the Thames and in Essex.

Of course, Caesar's tribute was never paid. Instead, a steady stream of pro-Roman British kings and politicians appeared as refugees in Rome imploring the emperors to intervene in Britain on their behalf. It seemed the Catuvellauni had become bullish again. But Caesar's immediate successors, Augustus and then Tiberius, had no expansionist ambitions at all as far as Britain was concerned. In the end it was left to the insane Caligua to attempt the first serious invasion.

In AD 39 - over 90 years after Caesar's last incursion - Caligua assembled a large army and fleet at Boulogne. Alas, the invasion plans misfired when the troops declined to obey embarkation instructions. In the face of this mutiny, all Caligua's generals could do was persuade the men to throw their javelins and shoot stones from their catapults into the sea, and fill their helmets with seashells. Mission completed, the emperor claimed a mighty victory over the ocean.

Two years later Caligua was murdered by his troops and replaced by his elderly uncle, Claudius.

Claudius boldly goes

Claudius was a thinking man by inclination and a scholar rather than a soldier, but he soon realised that in order to consolidate his position - some critics were still unconvinced of his worth - he needed the powerful and useful propaganda of a military victory. Britain was an obvious target. Rich in minerals and other raw materials, it was a potential refuge for troublemakers from Gaul. It was also there for the taking.

Head of a bronze statue of the emperor Claudius, found in the River Alde in Suffolk. Perhaps this was part of the loot of Boudicca's rebels from Colchester where the complete statue might have stood in the great temple.

In AD 43 he reconvened Caligua's invasion force somewhere on the French coast and placed the army under the command of Aulus Plautius. Having crossed the Channel, the fleet made an unopposed landing at Richborough in the north east corner of Kent.

It was a huge logistical undertaking and an enormous convoy, for the invasion force consisted of four legions - each a regiment of 6000 front line troops - and 20,000 to 30,000 auxiliaries. In all, nearly 50,000 men complete with stores, weapons and equipment.

With a beachead fort established Aulus Plautius and his troops stormed across north Kent, just as Caesar had done. They were unstoppable, and at a site beside the Thames, probably near Brentford, the British tribes under Caratacus and Togodumnus, kings of the Catuvellauni (who had finally won their struggle with the Trinovantes), were convincingly defeated.

The Roman advance was then deliberately halted to allow time for the emperor Claudius to arrive. And in due course he did, bringing with him a small army of his own and probably a number of elephants. Then, with Claudius at its head, the army of Rome marched into the old Celtic city of Camulodunum, modern Colchester, which at the time was capital of the combined kingdoms of the Catuvellauni and the Trinovantes.

Togodumnus was already dead, killed in the battle beside the Thames, and Caratacus had fled west. In effect, the Romans now commanded most of south east England.

Claudius's victory was marked in most suitable fashion in Rome by the erection of a great stone arch. After his death in AD 54 a huge classical temple with marble columns was also erected in Camulodunum to honour his spirit.

Early forts and the AD 47 revolt

The Romans spent four years establishing their army and strengthening control in the areas they had conquered. For one thing a substantial network of roads was constructed across southern and eastern England (described in No 2 of this series), with garrisons of Roman troops in timber forts spaced at intervals along them. The usual Roman garrison fort was square, covered about four acres and was surrounded by a pair of deep ditches around a rampart of turf and soil. A timber palisade and sentry-walk crowned the defences. Entry to the fort was through four gateways, one in the middle of each side, with timber towers and timber gates to guard it. Inside the fort long wooden barracks housed about 500 men and officers. In the case of cavalry forts the area would have been larger to allow room for stabling the horses.

Roman forces storming the Icenian stronghold to bring an end to the first revolt, in AD 47. This reconstruction is based on Holkham camp, one of the possible sites for the battle.

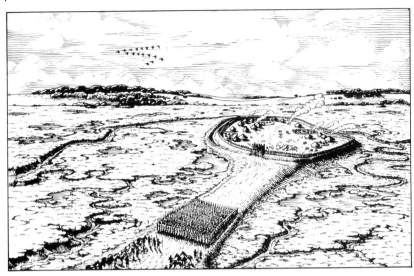

All these forts were virtually identical, so that a Roman soldier from one fort would be able to find his way around any other fort in Britain. The buildings were also of the same size and built by the same method of construction, so they could be erected from prefabricated portable sections. In the territory of the Iceni there were forts of this type and period at Threxton and Swanton Morley. There must have been others.

Changes were on the way, however. In AD 47 Aulus Plautius, who had by now become the first military governor, was replaced by another famous general, Ostorius Scapula. He brought with him firm instructions from Claudius to press ahead with the conquest of the island.

Pinpricks of defiance remained. Caratacus was still causing trouble, leading tribes from Wales and the west Midlands in raids across the "frontier" established by Plautius along the line of the Fosse Way between Exeter and Lincoln. In order to obtain men for his new campaign Scapula had to draw on the garrisons of the forts. Because of this, many of the tribal areas in the south east were left with no troops to keep an eye on them.

Scapula was aware of the problem, and thought he had a solution close to hand. He decided to enforce a Roman law, the *Lex Julia de Armis*, which effectively disarmed the men of conquered Britain. Its purpose was to deprive the tribes of their battle weapons; though they were allowed to carry weapons for hunting, and while travelling. His hope was that in this way his unguarded rear would be secure while he and his army moved off on a new campaign of conquest. It did not work out like that, however, for some of the more independent tribal spirits seem to have objected to the indignity. Among them was a faction of the Iceni who rose in open revolt. This is normally known as the first Iceni revolt, to distinguish it from the more wide ranging and somewhat better known rebellion under Boudicca.

Scapula, no doubt thoroughly irritated at this unexpected turn of events, finally sent a strong force against them. The Iceni retreated into a stronghold defended by earth banks, ditches and natural fortifications, and with a single line of approach along a narrow entrance.

This description, handed down by the Roman historian Tacitus, could be applied to a fort of this date at Stonea, then an isolated island in the middle of the Cambridgeshire fens. Equally, the description could also be applied to the Iron Age fort at Holkham, at the time in the middle of a vast expanse of tidal saltmarsh. Scapula, presumably anticipating a conventional battle, included a body of cavalry in his force. Faced by the defences of the Iceni stronghold, the Roman commander had no option but to order his cavalry to dismount. The fort was stormed on foot, and the rebellion quashed.

Tacitus made the incident sound very serious indeed - after all, it provided another overwhelming Roman victory - but other evidence suggests the revolt cannot have posed much of a threat. Soon after AD 47, for example, the Iceni were granted special privileges.

It is possible, therefore, the first revolt against Rome involved only one small section of the tribe.

Client kingdom

When Scapula finally marched into the west in AD 48 he left behind him an Iceni tribe ruled by a king named Prasutagus.

Until a few years' ago the only information relating to him was to be found in the writings of Tacitus and Dio. It was something of a puzzle that among the names inscribed on Iceni coins he was not mentioned at all. He seemed a very remote and barely perceived figure.

However, a detailed study of a series of Roman and Icenian silver coins found in a hoard at Joist Fen, Lakenheath, has shed more light. It showed that what at first had been seen as a nonsense inscription actually read SUBRIPRASTO on one side and ESICO FECIT on the other.

The second inscription is easy enough. It is Latin for "Esico made me." The other needs a little more deduction. The Celtic word for king was Ricon, so the inscription may be a Latin and Celtic mix meaning "under the king, Prasto", or "Prasutagus". If the two words do seem a trifle dissimilar it should be remembered that Prasutagus is a version of a Celtic name told to Tacitus and re-told by him in Latin. In any event, Prasto is the only reference so far found on a coin.

The coins themselves were different from the usual Iceni style. In fact the horse and head seem to suggest a closer artistic allegiance to Italy than to East Anglia. This fits very well with the notion of a pro-Roman king breaking away from Celtic traditions and producing coinage in the mould of his masters.

Prasutagus seems to have been what the Romans called a client king, in other words, the ruler of a "more or less" free kingdom on the edge of the empire. A client state had a great deal of independence, being able to retain many of its pre-conquest laws, institutions and coinage. Its freedom from external attack was guaranteed by Roman arms, and freedom from internal interference by Roman treaty.

In return, the king recognised that he ruled by courtesy of the emperor. Moreover, a king was expected to name the emperor as his heir. On the eventual death of the king the emperor would generously return power (normally, but not necessarily) to the king's natural successor.

It was an arrangement which had benefits for both sides, but it did sometimes lead to problems.

Another advantage for the Iceni client kingdom was an exemption from the taxes and tributes paid to Rome by other subjects of the empire.

Whatever the king and his people thought of the arrangement a brief, uneasy peace seems to have reigned after AD 47. Despite the brooding presence of the legions in the land life continued as normally as possible.

The move against the Druids

Scapula's campaigns in the late AD 40s, and those of his successors, brought southern England, the Midlands and Wales under Roman rule. The one exception was the north west corner of Wales -the Isle of Anglesey.

The island was a rallying point for resistance against Rome, and the Druids established a major centre there. Indeed, as religious and intellectual leaders of the British tribes they seem to have continued to lead opposition to Rome long after the political leaders had capitulated. They may also have attracted the last British warriors to the stronghold. In any event, final resistance was fanatical.

In AD 61 Suetonius Paulinus, by this time governor of the province of Britain, decided to rid the empire of this nuisance once and for all. Just as Scapula had done before him, he stripped many of the garrison forts of their troops and marched into Wales.

The Roman army reached the Menai Straits and glimpsed across the narrow channel the spectacle of hordes of determined warriors and wild priests. It was an atmosphere heightened by the reputation of the Druids for assorted atrocities, including the sacrifice of Roman prisoners. The Romans, for their part, must have sensed an opportunity for revenge.

Their army may have amounted to 20,000 troops. It certainly included elements of the 9th Legion from its fort at Longthorpe near Peterborough; and the complete 14th Legion, from the Midlands, the 20th (Gloucester), and additional auxiliary regiments.

Suetonius Paulinus picked his moment, ferried his men across the channel and defeated the Druidic army after a savage battle. The temples and sacred groves were burned and the last ember of British resistance crushed. It was a satisfying victory for Rome. Alas, at the very moment of triumph a messenger arrived from south east England with news so startling it was to bring Suetonius Paulinus scampering back from Anglesey.

Death of Prasutagus

It was the thin veneer of tranquility in the lands of the Iceni and their neighbours which gave Paulinus an opportunity to confront the Druids. He was reasonably confident his rear was secure, or at least quiet. However, at the time of the Anglesey campaign (circa AD 61), or shortly before, a devastating chain of events was set in motion by the death of Prasutagus.

The king of the Iceni seems to have been a wily politician. At some point he attempted, in his will, to save at least half of the kingdom for his own family by leaving only half to the emperor. Alas, the gamble misfired. By now Claudius was dead and replaced by the somewhat eccentric Nero. And Nero was not the sort to allow allies or subjects to get away with anything.

A silver coin, struck by Prasutagus, the Icenian king whose death sparked off Boudicca's revolt. Like the other Icenian coins, it shows a horse on one side. (Drawings based on photographs by Henry Mossop.)

Shortly after the death of Prasutagus a certain Catus Decianus, the Procurator, was sent to the royal centre of the Iceni. His job, as the official responsible for the finances of the Roman province of Britain, was to enforce Nero's authority by seizing the whole of the estate. The incident went sour, presumably because the Iceni, and particularly the king's widow, Boudicca, were reluctant to hand anything to the Roman intruders.

In the ensuing fracas Boudicca was beaten and her daughters raped by Roman soldiers.

It is not known where this incident took place. We can only guess that the tribal centre or royal palace may have been at Caistor St Edmund, later to become the Roman provincial capital, or at a different site altogether, perhaps in the Brecklands somewhere near Thetford.

In any event this was the incident which sparked a second catastrophic Iceni revolt.

Enter the queen

Boudicca is one of the first "real" people we perceive in Norfolk history, though the details which have been accumulated are very few indeed. All of them come from the writings of the Latin historian, Tacitus, and the Greek writer, Cassius Dio. Even then the accounts are incomplete. Nevertheless, they do open a tiny window on her life by illuminating some of the events of one short summer.

A certain amount of conjecture is possible, and necessary. Her husband could have died of natural causes, so she may not have been particularly young. It is known she had daughters, but not how many or how old they were. It is not known if she had any grown-up sons. This seems unlikely, otherwise they and not Boudicca would surely have led the revolt.

Perhaps we can imagine a woman in her late 30s or 40s, which at that time was a relatively advanced age; possibly the daughter of a royal house of another Iron Age tribe; but certainly a woman who, as the queen of Prasutagus, would have been accustomed to wielding authority and experienced in the ways of the Romans.

One general comment Roman historians did tend to make about Celtic women was that they were invariably involved in the running of the tribes and were very powerful figures, physically, socially and politically.

Cassius Dio provides the only known description of the queen. He speaks of her as a woman of "immense stature", though if set against the average size of the Mediterranean people of the day this does not mean she was necessarily huge. Even so, the Celts tended to be physically larger and stronger than most other tribes encountered by the Romans.

Boudicca was red haired (again, a common characteristic among Iron Age tribes) and she wore a great gold necklace and brightly coloured cloak.

It is not quite clear what Dio means by these comments, but it is nice to think she may have had around her neck a gold torc in the Snettisham tradition, worn not for decoration but as a symbol of her authority and power; and that her cloak was woven from wool dyed in red, green, blue and yellow, a formula which may have been a forerunner of the Scottish tartans.

Later events, of course, suggest that Boudicca was also capable of influencing large numbers of people, particularly fighting men, and more important, of keeping them together through a long campaign.

Iron and fire

According to Tacitus the revolt began as a direct result of the beating of Boudicca and the rape of her daughters. But there must have been more to it than this. It may also have been a last attempt by the Iceni to remain independent of Rome. They must have realised that with Prasutagus dead very little stood in the way of Nero annexing their lands as part of the Roman province of Britain.

In any event, when Boudicca called the warriors of the tribe to arms they flocked to her standard. And so the armed might of the Iceni finally poured down the road south, probably the Pye Road, the modern A140.

Colchester, the Roman capital, was the first target. Few Roman troops barred the way since most of the army was in Anglesey with Paulinus. Nevertheless, a detachment of the 9th Legion from Longthorpe near Peterborough did eventually move south east from its fort in a forlorn attempt to intercept.

Boudicca seems to have anticipated the manoeuvre by sending a portion of her forces ahead to prepare an ambush. The legionary troops were routed. In fact the Roman commander, Petilius Cerialis, was fortunate to escape with his life and a small detachment of cavalry.

At Longthorpe there are signs of a small fort having been built inside the main fort, and this may have been some sort of temporary stronghold built by Cerialis to guard against the possibility of "hot pursuit" by the Iceni. The real lesson of the ambush, however, is the clear indication of reliable tribal intelligence and the existence of an Iron Age scouting network.

Having disposed of the only readily available Roman forces the Iceni moved south again. Cerialis, realising the danger, despatched urgent messages to Paulinus in Anglesey and to the only other large force absent from the campaign, the 2nd Legion based in its fortress at Exeter under the command of Postumus, an elderly soldier on the verge of retirement.

Alas for Postumus, his nerve broke. Rather than commit his forces to a frantic dash across war-torn southern England he seems - according to Tacitus - to have locked the gates of the fortress and stayed secure within its walls until it was all over.

When the revolt was finally crushed the disgraced Postumus did the only honourable thing. He fell on his sword.

Before this, the triumphant Iceni reached Colchester where they were joined by the Trinovantes. The Trinovantes may have resented the amount of land seized from them to develop the Roman *colonia*, a settlement of veterans of the Roman army. The veterans, in turn, comprised a sort of elderly "home guard", available if trouble arose. Whether or not the Trinovantes did have a grudge against Rome they must have been excited by the sudden arrival on their doorstep of a huge and victorious army.

The city of Colchester was still under construction. No defences had been raised, one reason being that a great deal of time and effort had gone into the building of a large classical temple dedicated to the spirit of the dead Claudius. In the absence of walls the outnumbered defenders

A representation of the last stand in the Claudian temple at Colchester, as Boudicca's forces destroy the city.

retreated to the solid surroundings of the temple. Here they fought doggedly, holding out for a time.

In the end, however, the temple was taken and its defenders butchered. Colchester was razed to the ground, and surviving Romans and known Roman sympathisers massacred.

The debris of this disaster has been detected in many of the excavations conducted in Colchester. Thick layers of charred wood, clay walls baked hard in the fire, and piles of rubble from demolished buildings are common finds. In some places the heat was so intense cups and bowls melted and ran into puddles of molten glass.

Boudicca's next target was London, a small and relatively new settlement which began to grow in the early years of Roman rule. It received exactly the same treatment as Colchester.

Dio and Tacitus both paint a particularly lurid picture of the massacre of the inhabitants of London. It seems the warriors of the Iceni indulged in an orgy of bloodletting of a sort few army commanders of any period have been able to control. The ferocity was partly inspired by tribal resentment and partly, perhaps, by the few Druids who had not withdrawn to Anglesey. In the face of Rome's all-out attack on their religion, Druids and tribal leaders alike would have been able to whip their men into a religious and patriotic frenzy. In the event the looting, raping and pillaging left London deserted and in flames.

Paulinus, in receipt of the message from Cerialis, was by this time galloping south with his cavalry along the line of Watling Street, the modern A5. He arrived in sight of London in time to witness its destruction, but his immediate forces may have numbered hundreds rather than thousands. Clearly he could not hope to match the British horde.

Now we see Paulinus as the great tactician. He withdrew back along Watling Street with Boudicca's army baying at his heels. They poured through the Roman city of Verulamium (modern St Albans), which suffered exactly the same fate as Colchester and London. Paulinus, however, was simply luring the enemy into an area he had already scouted, and where he had chosen to make his stand.

For the first time since the bloody revolt began Paulinus was beginning to take control of the situation. From this point on he dictated all the moves.

Leaving Verulamium far behind his strategic withdrawal took him back along the line of Watling Street into the Midlands and on to the battle site, probably at Mancetter in Warwickshire. Here he rendezvoused with the main body of his force which had marched at infantry speed all the way from Anglesey.

Making good use of the terrain Paulinus calmly ranged them in line of battle to confront Boudicca's gathering army.

An Icenian warrior ready for battle.
His sword scabbard is based on one
found at Congham, and parts of his
shield on pieces from a hoard of
bronzework from Ringstead.

Arms and the men

The armies which confronted each other at Mancetter were equipped for and schooled in two quite different ways of fighting.

The ordered discipline of the Roman forces was in complete contrast to the unrestrained and flamboyant attitude of the Celts. A warrior of the Iceni was used to fighting as an individual rather than as a small cog in a large military machine. He was also equipped with the weapons and armour of the Iron Age.

His helmet was of thin bronze plate mounted on thick leather padding. Most of the rest of his body was unprotected by metal armour, though protection of sorts was afforded by stout leather trousers.

Julius Caesar also wrote that the Celts covered their bodies with a blue dye made from the woad plant. It seems likely they actually tattooed themselves with elaborate designs using woad extract as a medium for the tattoo. There is some evidence of this. The bodies of Scythians, close cousins of the Celts, found preserved in the deep frost of the Siberian tundra, had just these sort of tattoos on their frozen skins.

Woad, incidentally, was used as a dye for cloth until the 18th and 19th centuries when it slowly went out of fashion with the arrival of indigo.

The Iron Age warrior also sought to protect himself with a shield, a wooden, leather or bronze oval which reached from chin to knees and had sufficient width to cover the body. Most examples which have survived are of thin bronze with embellishments of enamel, coral (imported from the Near East, probably the Red Sea), or a substitute for coral made out of chalk and stained red.

Iron Age sword, made of iron, found in a grave at Shouldham. The hilt is made in the form of a human figure.

In one case a shield found in the river Witham in Lincolnshire originally carried the figure of a wild boar cut out of leather and rivetted to the bronze. Later, this was removed and replaced with elaborate bronze bosses.

Most of the bronze was less than a millimetre thick and would never have survived a sustained attack from iron weapons. It is assumed, therefore, that most shields were intended for display and parade purposes and not for battle, and that during actual fighting the warrior used a shield made from wood or leather, as the sagas of Iron Age warriors in Ireland describe.

His offensive weapons were the sword and the spear. Though they are frequently mentioned in the Irish poems and by Roman writers, few spears have survived. However, they seem to have been large iron spearheads mounted on shafts of ash wood 7ft or 8ft long, and may have resembled a pikestaff.

Most devastating weapon of all was the sword, a great flat double-edged iron blade 3ft long. Made for hacking rather than stabbing it had very little point but boasted an elaborate hilt which carried bone or wooden plate decorations, and often an enamelled bronze pommel. It hung at the warrior's hip or down his back in a scabbard of wood, leather or bronze, which was also carefully ornamented with enamel, inserts of coral, or flowing incised patterns.

These swords fascinated the Romans, and many Latin historians commented on their size and weight which contrasted with the shorter and lighter standard issue sword used by the Roman army.

One writer, remarking that Iron Age swords were strong and not liable to break, also pointed out they were made of a slightly soft metal. He went on to explain that if two Iron Age warriors were involved in single combat their swords would eventually begin to bend. At a mutually convenient moment they would step back, straighten their swords over their knees, and then recommence where they had left off.

The authors are tempted to suggest the tradition of English "sportsmanship" and "fair play" might have begun here!

In any event the swords were prized possessions and the only pieces of Iron Age weaponry the makers inscribed with any sort of signature. Some have names stamped on them. Others have trademarks such as the figure of a pig or a bear.

Celtic warriors, of course, were of high social status, and only wealthy or important men could afford to purchase the weapons of war or expect them to be supplied by the chief. By and large war seems to have been an exclusive preoccupation of the upper and monied classes. The mass of the peasants was neither armed nor expected to fight.

The battle taxi

The most costly and prestigious piece of equipment of all was the chariot, and it seems likely that only a small portion of the upper echelons of society owned these examples of Celtic high technology. They were not the lumbering waggons portrayed by Hollywood and by Victorian romanticists, but light, fast wooden carts with slender spoked wheels and lightweight wickerwork panels for sides. They were pulled by a pair of small ponies harnessed by a wooden yoke and central shaft.

Again, the trappings of chariot and ponies were of bronze and like the rest of the warrior's equipment elaborately decorated with enamel and engraved patterns. Reins passed from bronze bits in the ponies' mouths through terret rings on the yoke to the dashboard of the chariot. This prevented the reins from tangling and dropping among the ponies' legs. Linchpins of bronze or iron held the wheels on the axle. The wheel, in turn, was kept in shape by an iron tyre and by a nave hoop around the hub.

It is a system used by agricultural wheelwrights until well into the present century.

For the sake of lightness and speed most of the chariot was made out of wood, for they were not tanks but fast personnel carriers used to take a single warrior into battle.

Driven by a charioteer, probably a slave or servant, there would have been very little room for the warrior and his equipment. Nevertheless, when battle was joined the charioteer carried his master into the thick of the fray. The warrior dismounted and the charioteer withdrew to a safe distance. Once fighting was over the warrior, if he survived, recalled his chariot and was driven off again.

Above all, Iron Age chariots were for display. When Julius Caesar first encountered them in 54 BC he was amazed by the antics of the Celtic warriors. He relates how at the beginning of a battle individual champions exhibited themselves like prizefighters in front of the armies in brash displays of finery and "braggadocio". Sometimes this simply consisted of standing and waving weapons in the air. But Caesar also saw the chariots used in another context.

Warriors were driven up and down in the space between the waiting armies, and then performed feats of agility to demonstrate their skill and nimbleness. They would run up the chariot shaft (no mean feat at top speed) to the yoke across the ponies' shoulders and then, as the ponies galloped across the battlefield, swing themselves down on to the ground, spring on to the ponies' backs, and even turn somersaults to return to the chariot.

It sounds more like Buffalo Bill's wild west show than the serious business of warfare, and it underlines two totally different styles of approach.

The professionals

In terms of attitude, equipment and the way in which he fought, the Roman soldier was a very different proposition indeed.

The crack front line troops were the legions, regiments of nominally 6000 men, each designed as a self-contained battle unit with its own officers, supply systems, craftsmen (blacksmiths, leatherworkers, engineers) and a small number of horsemen.

The legion was essentially an infantry machine which fought as a single entity.

According to Roman law each man was supposed to be a minimum of 5ft 6in tall, although a number of skeletons found in graves of the period suggest a portion of the civilian population, and thus some of the troops, may have been somewhat shorter. At the same time they were enormously fit and as tough as any soldiers who have fought in any army.

Originally, only the citizens of the city of Rome were eligible to join, but qualification was later softened and extended to the whole of Italy. At the time of the Boudiccan revolt, for example, the legions were open to any man who could claim the distinction of Roman citizenship. This would have included all the male inhabitants of Italy and those of many cities scattered through parts of the empire. So the legionaries themselves would have been very mixed bunch, speaking Latin and in some cases a native language, too, such as Spanish or Gallic.

They were all volunteers who, on joining up, were paid a bounty from which they had to purchase their equipment and pay for transportation to the current base of the legion to which they had been assigned.

Term of service was for 20 years. If they survived, they would end as veterans and be rewarded with a plot of land in a *colonia*, a city peopled by Roman citizens in the midst of the "foreign" population of a province. In Britain, Colchester was a city of this sort.

The actual state of the Roman army at the time of the Boudiccan revolt was as it had been left following the military reforms of Marius over a century earlier. Sometimes the legionaries were known insultingly as "Marius's mules", as every man in the line had to carry a prodigious 60 lb of equipment on his shoulders. This was the standard issue pack of food (primarily cereal which was cooked and eaten as a sort of gruel, a ration of sour wine for drinking), blanket, wooden stakes (used for fortifying the camp built at the end of every day's march), and weapons.

A soldier from a Roman legion examines his pilum (javelin) before going on parade.

All the heaviest equipment, including leather tents large enough to house 12 men, were loaded on waggons which formed the inevitable baggage train. The essence of military thinking was that every man had to be self-contained in case the baggage train was left behind in a forced march.

On his head the Roman soldier wore a helmet of iron or bronze fitted with leather padding to provide some sort of fit, and with a small socket on top to hold a brightly coloured plume for ceremonial or full dress parades. Next to his skin was a skirted tunic reaching from his shoulders to just above his knees, and over this a breastplate which was a miracle of Roman ingenuity.

Instead of a rigid shell, like medieval armour, the Roman breastplate, called a *lorica segmentata*, more closely resembled a lobster shell made of thin steel strips which overlapped each other and so allowed the body a degree of flexibility. The strips were joined by leather straps, while on the left side of the body they were linked by bronze hinges. On the right hand side the breastplate was fastened round the chest by straps and buckles. Another set of strips, running from back to front across the shoulders, completed the armour.

Around his waist the infantryman wore a thick leather belt studded with bronze plates from which, at the front, hung a heavy leather "apron", again studded with metal plates. On his feet he wore heavy leather hobnailed sandals, and according to some military documents, thick woolly socks.

The defensive gear was completed by a great shield made out of plywood with a edging of bronze and a large iron boss in the centre.

Offensive equipment comprised two different types of weapon. For long range work the infantryman carried two javelins, or *pila*, each about 6ft 6in long. These were heavy wooden shafts topped with a head made out of iron and steel. The actual point was made of hard steel, but the section between shaft and point was deliberately made of a somewhat softer iron so that the javelin actually bent if it struck an enemy either on a shield or on the body. The purpose of this was to prevent the javelin being thrown back at the Roman army.

After the battle, which the Romans naturally assumed they would win, the blacksmiths toured the field and collected the *pila* which were then straightened at the forges and re-issued to the troops.

The most important weapon of all was the sword, the *gladius*. This was designed for a stabbing attack. It closely resembled a large carving knife less than 18in long and with a sharp point. Made of steel, with bone or wooden plates on the handle to afford a secure grip it was, like the shield, sometimes "customised" with engraved or painted decoration on the steel or wood.

A soldier particularly keen to make an impression on his comrades, or who had come into money, might commission a special sword from a manufacturer. This would be very handsome indeed. Most weapons, however, were plain standard issue swords made in military workshops and sold by the army to its new recruits.

The legionaries lived under a harsh regime of strict discipline in which punishments for offences ranged from extra duties to flogging or even death.

In the extreme case of mutiny, or a complete legion displaying cowardice, the ultimate sanction was decimation in which one man in ten, selected by lot, would be executed and the legion then reformed.

Discipline was enforced through a chain of command leading from the commanding officer, the *legatus*, through his junior officers, the *tribunes* - often young politicians working their way up the ladder of power - to the centurions, the non-commissioned officers. These were men of 10 or 15 years' service who had risen through the ranks, and each of whom was responsible for about one hundred men, the equivalent of a company in the modern army.

This was the most important unit for fighting and for administration. The second line troops, the auxiliaries, were recruited from those parts of the empire where the people were not citizens of Rome. They served under conditions similar to those of the legionaries, and on discharge were awarded Roman citizenship. This meant, of course, that the son of an auxiliary veteran could serve in the legions.

Most auxiliary regiments were allowed to retain their national characteristics, and they fought with the traditional weapons of the country in which they were first levied. Thus the specialist fighters of the Roman army -the cavalrymen, archers, slingers, and a few infantry units armed in a different way to the legions - were all auxiliaries.

However, the auxiliaries and their equipment and methods were generally regarded as second rate and fit only to be used in support of the legions. Their standing might be seen as similar to county regiments being used in support of the Brigade of Guards.

The military machine

The Roman army fought in disciplined units, and its organisation and regime allowed considerable co-ordination in battle. This undoubtedly contributed to its success. In some ways the Romans were the originators of modern military tactics and many generals, including Napoleon, modelled their army systems on those of Rome.

The legions would fight in a line six ranks deep and a thousand men wide. When battle was joined, and at the officers' commands, javelins were hurled at the enemy in two devastating volleys. The resulting confusion often caused the enemy to drop their shields, at which point the legions would draw swords and, holding their own shields in front of them in a solid wall, they would charge in strict formation and at a measured pace.

The sight of Roman swords sticking from the edges of compact lines of advancing shields must have had a considerable effect. The physical impact of 6000 men each covered with 50lbs or so of armour would have been considerable.

In many cases the disciplined swordsmanship of the legionaries was enough to finish the job quickly and professionally. The auxiliaries, guarding the flanks while the archers and cavalrymen harried the enemy from a distance, cleared the battlefield and mopped up after the legions had done the donkey work and grabbed the glory.

All this was in sharp contrast to the individualistic attitude and tactics adopted by Celtic warriors like the Iceni. For them, battle provided more of an occasion for display and prestige than for actually killing people. In consequence, and once confronted by the cast iron order of the Roman army, there was little doubt about the outcome.

The trap closes

The balance sheet of strengths and weaknesses between his own army and that of Boudicca must have occupied Paulinus' mind during the initial dash along Watling Street. He already knew that the bulk of his forces could not hope to reach Colchester, London or St Albans before the Iceni. He must, however, have been confident of victory in any setpiece battle.

It is possible, therefore, that he kept a lookout for a suitable place where he might fight on his terms.

On his way down Watling Street during the race from Anglesey he may have seen the ideal spot, a range of hills offering a clear space with a thick wood behind and on either side, and a high view of where Watling Street crossed a river in a wide marshy valley.

This, in any event, is how Tacitus described the site. It is a description matched very closely by a spot near Mancetter.

In any event Paulinus seems to have lured the Iceni back along Watling Street to the very spot where he had instructed the bulk of his troops to wait for him. By the time the Iceni arrived they would have gazed up the slope and seen the Roman army waiting above them in battle formation, with one or possibly two legions in the centre and the auxiliary cavalry on either side. The auxiliary infantry were held behind in reserve.

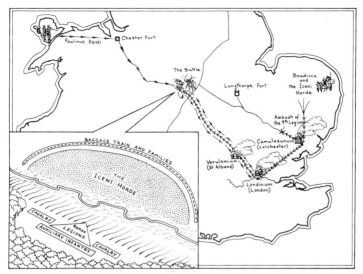

The military campaign of AD 61, showing the rampaging Boudicca and the movements of the Roman forces. Inset is a reconstruction of the final battle near Mancetter (with grateful acknowledgements to Dr. Graham Webster who worked it all out).

With thick woodland on either side and behind the Romans, the Iceni were left with no alternative but to mount a frontal attack. To do this they had to struggle across the marshes and through the river. The Iceni horde (to call it a disciplined army would be an exaggeration), slowed by its baggage train carrying loot and the women and children, nevertheless began to move forward.

It was at this point the Roman machine slipped into gear. Two flights of javelins hurtled through the air. Though they may not have accounted for large numbers of warriors they would, nevertheless, have caused confusion and made the attack falter.

The soft, marshy ground added to the problems of the Iceni, and it seems likely that when Paulinus finally slipped his legions off the leash Boudicca was not properly prepared to meet the attack.

Whether this was the case or not, the movement of perhaps 10,000 battle-hardened troops in a solid line of wood, steel and sinew, and the initial shock of the charge, may well have decided the course and ultimate outcome of the battle.

The Iceni broke, gave way immediately (according to Tacitus), turned and ran. Now the retreat was hampered by the numbers behind them, by the wet ground, and by the baggage train. In the confusion the legions, with the auxiliary troops in close support, moved forward and slaughtered all within reach. When the Iceni tried to scatter and flee they were chased and cut down by the cavalry and infantry. The Roman victory was complete.

Tacitus also tells us - from the standpoint of the victor, of course - that 80,000 Iceni and allies were killed at a cost of 400 Romans. This may be an overstatement. The total size of the opposing armies at the beginning of the battle is uncertain. Again, Tacitus would like us to believe that the British fielded almost a quarter of a million men against a Roman force which probably numbered about 10,000 legionaries and perhaps a similar number of auxiliaries. Again, the figures may be distorted.

The impression remains, however, of an overwhelming defeat for Boudicca.

In the confusion and aftermath of battle many of the surviving Iceni and their allies presumably fled and attempted to return to their homes. For Boudicca, though, the campaign was over, and she fades from view.

The actual details of her fate are uncertain. Tacitus says she committed suicide. Cassius Dio wrote that she died of an illness. The implication is that although she may have survived the battle she may not have lived for very long afterwards.

There are many reports and rumours as to her final resting place, including sites ranging from Garboldisham to Hampstead Heath and King's Cross railway station. None of them have any real substance. Given the circumstances of the battle and its outcome it is quite likely her body was buried hurriedly but lavishly and the grave gradually forgotten. In any event no trace has ever come to light.

Even in defeat Boudicca remains one of East Anglia's greatest and most potent heroines emerging, rightly or wrongly, as a symbol of a struggle for freedom. Few other local characters have taken such a solid hold on the imagination of succeeding generations.

Punishment and peace

Once the excitement of battle and victory had passed the immediate task facing Paulinus was to settle accounts with the surviving Iceni. Many were still alive, of course, and despite ghastly casualty figures must have fled the field and made their way home.

The army of Rome undoubtedly followed, and although no details have emerged it is not unreasonable to suppose that other tribes had also joined in the revolt, including some of the Trinovantes from around Colchester, and Paulinus would have punished them too. Property may have been confiscated, houses destroyed and animals taken away and sold in the markets or used as army rations.

If there were any sections of the tribe which had not joined with Boudicca, or were able to convince the Romans they had been forced to participate against their will, then Paulinus no doubt showed them favour and raised them to positions of authority within the tribal system.

It would have provided the authorities with a friendly power base and is, of course, a tactic conquerors everywhere have employed.

In any event there is no record of any further fighting. It must be assumed that the collapse of the revolt and of armed resistance against Rome was total.

Assuming Paulinus had moved into East Anglia with his entire force, which included units from the 9th, 14th and 20th legions, and auxiliary troops, then we may speculate that he would have wanted to move them out again as soon as possible, leaving only his auxiliaries in garrison forts to keep an eye on things for a time.

Paulinus was faced with a very real problem. On the one hand he needed to punish the Iceni - and wanted to let the rest of Britain know he was doing so - while on the other he wanted the tribe to retain sufficient wealth and production capacity to pay Roman taxes. In other words, there was nothing to be gained from the total destruction of this Iron Age society.

Tacitus does remark, somewhat unusually, that the Roman army stayed *"sub pellibus."* This might be described as "under canvas." More accurately it means, "under leather." Either way, the troops spent the winter shivering in leather tents in temporary forts rather than in the more usual permanent forts. This implies either that the punishment of the Iceni occurred so late in the season there was no time to build permanent forts before the onset of winter, or more likely, that Paulinus intended to leave troops in Norfolk no longer than was absolutely necessary.

If he did expect to be able to withdraw the legions in AD 62 then this could mean only one thing - that there was a friendly local faction who could be trusted to run the tribe and the territory for Rome.

Little is known of how the territory was actually garrisoned, though one temporary fort, known as a marching camp, has been identified at Horstead near the present bridge over the river Bure at Coltishall.

The camp was large enough to hold about 5000 men and would have been thrown up at the end of a day's march ready for a single night's stay. This was normal practice for an army moving through hostile country, and there must have been well established and frequently rehearsed drills to ensure that these camps were built in the shortest possible time. Every man must have had a clearly defined role.

Marching camps such as the one at Horstead were surrounded by a ditch, the dug soil being piled on the inside to form a rampart. They were rectangular in shape with an entrance in the middle of each of the four sides. Once the ditch was dug and the rampart built a palisade of timber stakes was erected along the top. Each soldier carried a stake among his kit for this very task. Only when the defences were finished, of course, could the huge leather tents be deployed and rations cooked for supper.

There must be many camps of this type waiting to be found in Norfolk.

More substantial forts would also have been built, and several of these are known. At Pakenham, in Suffolk, for example, excavations in 1984/85 by the Suffolk Archaeological Unit showed that cropmarks spotted on aerial photographs belonged to a Roman fort of this date. Some Norfolk sites, such as Threxton, may also belong to this period, but it is difficult to be certain without large scale excavation.

Fison Way mystery

There is one site where we do know the Roman army was operating at this time. This is the huge and puzzling complex at Gallows Hill on the Fison Way industrial estate at Thetford.

Here, between 1980 and 1982, excavations by the Norfolk Archaeological Unit uncovered the remains of an Iron Age settlement. This may have begun as early as 200 BC in the form of a farming village on the Icknield Way overlooking the ford across the Little Ouse river in the modern town in the valley below.

At some point before the conquest of AD 43 the village was replaced by an extraordinary complex in the form of a pair of deep ditches surrounding a square enclosure, about an acre in extent, which contained a large and elaborate timber building.

An interpretation of this site is difficult. The degree of elaboration suggests an important tribal centre, perhaps even the palace of Prasutagus himself. But if this was the headquarters of the client king then he would surely have lived in comfort and received luxury goods from the empire including, for example, wine in large amphorae, Samian pottery from France, or fine glass vessels. Nothing of this was found. Indeed, little debris of any kind was discovered.

It makes it hard to believe the site was ever used for habitation. An alternative theory is that the great timber building was not a house but a temple, and that the site was visited only on special religious occasions or lived-in permanently by just a few resident priests. This idea is strengthened by the fact that some 200 years later a Roman temple was built about 50 yards away. This is where the famous Thetford Treasure of gold and silver was found. The hilltop, therefore, may have had some special significance.

Plan and reconstruction drawing of the Icenian site at Fison Way, Thetford, as it would have looked just before the revolt of Boudicca in AD 61. An aerial photograph of the site today can be found on Page 4.

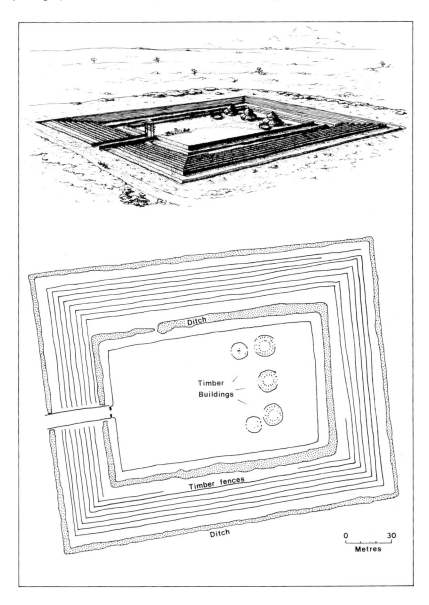

None of this helps to pinpoint where Prasutagus and Boudicca did have their capital, or indeed, what it was like. On the south coast near Chichester another client king, Cogidumnus, had a palace built at Fishbourne very much in the Roman style and richly appointed by Roman architects and builders. It may have been some sort of diplomatic gift. Alas, nothing of the sort has been found in Norfolk. Indeed, nothing remotely like it has been found anywhere in the lands of the Iceni.

Something even more extraordinary was to happen to the Gallows Hill site, however. Between the first Roman conquest of Britain and Boudicca's revolt, a third ditch was dug around the outside to enclose an area of about eleven acres, or the size of a small football stadium. In addition, the gap between the new and earlier ditches, something like 30 yards, was filled with a complex entanglement of enormous timber fences.

If the posts were 6ft tall then the total length of timber used was an astounding 70 miles.

The area outside the enclosure was also used at the time. About 30 long narrow pits, between six and seven feet long, two to three feet wide and two to three deep were dug in small groups, some of them surrounded by circular gullies. They look for all the world like graves, but the soil on the hill is so acid that any bone would have been eaten away. So we assume that there was a cemetery outside the great enclosure.

What was inside this site is uncertain. Perhaps the interior was simply left empty. If so this may have been intentional, in which case the site may have been some sort of stadium for open air ceremonies.

The redesign of the site was clearly to give more space inside, which was doubled in size. On either side of the circular building a new one was built, giving a line of three great circular houses across the enclosure. In front of each of the new ones stood a small circular area, surrounded by a low clay wall. We cannot begin to imagine what these were for, perhaps some mysterious ritual. Between the buildings and the entrance, which consisted of a fenced corridor through the rows of massed fence posts, was a large open space, perhaps intended for open-air ceremonies.

Yet another explanation of the empty central area is that building construction was halted by the rebellion of AD 61, and the site never completed.

Whatever the explanation, Paulinus would have found the construction sitting atop a strategic hill on an important line of communication overlooking a key river crossing. It was also a site which could be defended if trouble did break out and one which, if it was a religious centre, was an important focus for the defeated tribe. It is possible it also solved another of his problems - a lack of timber supplies for his own forts. The fences would have yielded huge quantities which may have been carted away and used in Roman building work elsewhere.

A few pieces of Roman military equipment, including hinges and buckles from a breastplate, were found during the excavation. It is possible these were lost by soldiers demolishing or supervising the demolition of the main structure.

This Thetford site is the most elaborate example of a series of smaller square enclosures, each about an acre in size, which have been found in various parts of north and north west Norfolk including Wighton, Warham (in the field next to the Camp) and Thornham.

They seem to have been built in the late Iron Age or early Roman period, but there are few clues as to their original purpose.

Enter the arbitrator

Paulinus seems to have been careful not to bleed the Iceni dry.

Nevertheless, there were a number of complaints from the people of Britain alleging excessive zeal. Indeed, there seems to have been dispute between Paulinus, the military governor, and Julius Classicianus, the procurator or financial controller.

Eventually the dispute and the complaints reached the ears of the emperor and Nero responded by sending one of his civil servants, a Greek named Polycleitus, to act as arbiter and to settle the argument. This he did at a public event at which the two men figuratively shook hands and declared the matter solved. It seemed to be the end of the matter. A few weeks or months later, however, Paulinus was replaced as governor of Britain on the pretext that some Roman ships had been lost off the British coast in unexplained circumstances.

The new governor seems to have been rather more in the mould of Classicianus, and we hear of no more complaints to Rome. Indeed, when Classicianus died a huge tombstone was erected to his memory by his wife and the citizens of Britain as a token of their gratitude for the way in which he had tempered the military harshness of Paulinus.

Quite by chance the tombstone survives. Having first been set up in a cemetery in Roman London it was demolished some 200 years later and used to build part of the Roman riverside wall along the southern edge of the Thames. These re-used fragments were subsequently uncovered again, and are now in the British Museum.

This point in the story marks the real end of the Iron Age in Norfolk, and indeed, the end of any lingering aspirations of independence some of the Iceni may have harboured. The Roman period was now firmly established, and peace returned to the countryside. Great historical events were all but over, and there followed three centuries of prosperity which we will deal with as separate subjects rather than in any particular chronological order.

The new order

Once military matters had been attended to the Roman authorities turned their minds to re-organising the tribe in such a way it would fit quickly and comfortably into the imported administrative system.

In the end matters were something of a compromise in that, traditionally, the conquerors liked to leave things much as they were when the tribes were free. On the other hand they wanted to make sure nothing remained to give potential rebels any sort of focus for future resistance.

Long before the conquest the Iceni had been a self-governing tribe with kings or noble rulers. There is no reason why the same thing did not happen under the heel of Rome. Thus the tribe became the unit of local government, substantially self-directing but under the firm general control of the governor in London. In this way local government units tended to be run by local worthies whose ancestors, in the case of the Iceni, may have been tribal warriors or whose fathers or grandfathers fought in Boudicca's army.

Once this framework was established the Iceni aristocracy quickly realised the best thing they could do was co-operate with the governor and the new order.

It is not known how the transition was made from martial law (which presumably existed for the first few years after the revolt) to a completely civil administration, but such a system may have been established within 15 years or so, perhaps by AD 75 or 80.

It could have been done by imposing on the tribe a *praefectus civitatis*, a military commissioner responsible to the Roman governor in London, charged with the task of overseeing an orderly transition of the administration into a civilian bureaucracy.

Although there is no precise information about the Iceni there is evidence from elsewhere that the usual means was to establish a local council, or *ordo*, which seems to have fulfilled much the same function as a modern county council. The big difference, however, was that the Romano British *ordo* was not elected but coerced.

All townsmen who owned more than a certain amount of property or a certain amount of wealth were forced to serve. Not only did they have to attend meetings and take decisions, but each was allocated a job in the public services, such as the maintenance of roads, bridges, water supplies or sewers.

All the expenses of repairing the roads or re-piping water mains came out of the councillors' own pockets! It goes without saying it was an unpopular role. Indeed, wealthy Iceni men who owned property in the rural areas may have escaped the duty. This could have been a good reason for avoiding town life. On the other hand anyone who did avoid it also sacrificed any real social standing and soon became out of touch with the latest whims and fashions.

Incidentally, there was no room within the Roman system for Iceni women to exercise anywhere near the sort of power which Boudicca had enjoyed in her day.

A puppet government

There is no indication of how many years passed between the repression of the Iceni after the revolt and the establishment of a peaceful and prosperous system. There must have been a transitional stage, but whether long or troublesome is not known.

Of course, there is every chance some members of the tribe had at best been lukewarm in their support of the revolt and these are the sort of people who would have stepped forward to help the authorities with the re-structuring of government and the settling of old scores. If this was the case the new order may have been established quickly, and it is possible to imagine a local council running the tribe - backed by the Roman military authorities - within three to four years.

The new local government would have needed a seat, the equivalent of a county town, and historians know from later references by Roman writers and geographers that the choice finally fell on Caistor St Edmund, a few miles south of present-day Norwich. In fact the name of the new town, Venta Icenorum, gives it away immediately, as in each Roman "county" only one township - the "county" town - carried the name of the tribe living there.

It is therefore assumed the *ordo* of Venta held sway over most of the old Iceni tribal territory, including parts of north Suffolk down as far as Bury St Edmunds.

Providing they operated within the strict framework of Roman law, and kept the administration running smoothly, then local councils seem to have been left to get on with the job. Any departure from the system, however, earned a stern rebuke from London or even from Rome.

Choosing the county town

A decision on a site for the new county capital was probably taken within the first year or two after the revolt. But why Caistor?

It does have some natural geographical recommendations. For example, it sits at the side of the valley of a river, the Tas, which may have been large enough to allow medium-sized boats to bring in trade goods and supplies from the coastal ports. It was also a good centre for communications, being to the north and on the outside of the heavy clay lands which would have been wet and impassable most winters. Caistor was also far enough up the Yare/Wensum river system to allow roads radiating from Caistor to cross rivers with relative ease.

Even so, there must have been hundreds of similar spots which would have done just as well. Why, for example, did they not choose the site on which Norwich grew a few hundred years later?

In the end the deciding factor may have been that there was already some sort of Icenian settlement at Caistor.

All in all the alternative explanations for the choice of site seem to be:

a) That Caistor was a "green fields" site with nothing around it before the Roman town was built, deliberately chosen by the authorities to distance the new administration from the old power centres of the tribe which had supported Boudicca. This explanation is attractive because although Iceni coins have been found in and around Caistor there are no known remains of a major pre-Roman settlement.

b) That there was a major pre-Roman settlement (location still to be discovered) and that the Romans simply decided to continue to use the same centre and "Romanize" it. This seems unlikely, but possible future discoveries such as an Iceni township might alter the theory.

c) That there was a settlement at Caistor, not the old tribal centre, perhaps, but the seat of a local group which supported the Romans during the revolt, or which had been half-hearted in its support of Boudicca and was thus rewarded by being made the new county town ahead of the tribal capital, which may have been on the other side of Norfolk in the Brecklands.

Of the three, the latter seems the most plausible explanation at the moment.

Building the county town

The instruction to begin building would have been given by the governor, but as Roman governors tended to change at regular intervals it is not known who was responsible.

In any event Roman surveyors, with all their wealth of experience of the regular layouts of the forts and camps, were involved in the initial planning and layout of the town. The final design showed the normal Roman pattern of a grid system of streets defining a series of square or rectangular blocks known as *insulae* which were laid out, if not actually built, as the first operation.

The street plan of the original Venta Icenorum covered a much larger area than that subsequently enclosed by the town walls built in the 4th

The Roman county town, Venta Icenorum (Caistor St Edmund). On the plan the grid pattern of streets (stippled) runs under and beyond the late Roman wall and ditch. On the photo the four sides of the walled town are marked by trees and bushes, and the street grid by the pale cropmarks where the grass was parched in the drought of 1977.
(Photo: Derek A. Edwards, Norfolk Archaeological Unit, 1977.)

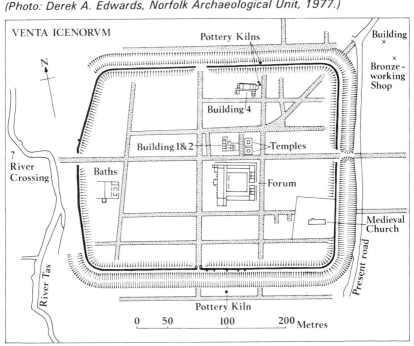

century AD, and it does look as if the original concept proved too ambitious. Local resources, or local needs, do not seem to have matched what the authorities first had in mind.

The usual pattern in Romano British towns was for shops, houses and workshops to be built of timber in the first few years, only to be reconstructed in stone if and when the prosperity of the town increased. Most of these buildings were privately owned. There is certainly no indication they were built by central government, but instead, by someone who bought a plot of land and decided to work or live on it.

Although the layout of the street grid was official government policy, the way in which the *insulae* were filled with buildings seems to have been a matter for individual landowners acting without any sort of planning control. There is a slight parallel here with the way in which the *ordo* administered its own business within general guidelines laid down by the Roman authorities.

The transition from timber to stone may therefore have been piecemeal, with individual buildings being improved as the prosperity of the owner increased. It is likely the process lasted many decades.

The private landscape

The sites of two stone houses inside the street pattern which may have been privately owned are known. One of these comprised a large range of living rooms and small workshops with a yard at the rear where the owner seems to have been involved in metalworking and the making of glass.

This is the only evidence for glassmaking in Roman Britain. It is possible, of course, that the workshops produced only window glass. Fine glassware, including cups and bottles, seems to have been imported from elsewhere in the empire.

Part of the living quarters of this house had a floor of tesserae, in this case small cubes of red brick laid as a single plain floor with none of the elaborate embellishments of mosiac floors seen in other towns.

This building, and all the others excavated in the town, were revealed by the excavations of Donald Atkinson which took place in 1929 and 1935 after a grid of streets was spotted on an RAF photograph taken in the drought summer of 1928. The picture aroused so much public interest that funds were subscribed to allow Atkinson to investigate a portion of the remains. Because the excavation took place so long ago when archaeology was still a young science the evidence is sometimes inadequate by modern standards.

Owing to continual modern agricultural activity little is known about the house above foundation level. It is not even known if the superstructure was of flint or of timber resting on stone foundations, after the style of many later houses in Norfolk villages.

The second house at Caistor, known as Building 4, was rather more domestic in character. There is no evidence of any sort of industrial activity, although there had been pottery kilns on the spot, probably in the late 1st century AD before the house was built. Traces of these had been covered and largely swept away before the house was built. This building gives an impression of wealth and some comfort, for heating was provided in one part by a hypocaust, an underfloor heating system. It may have been the dwelling of one of the council members whose wealth was derived from country estates some distance from the town, but who kept a town house and therefore had to serve his term of office on the council.

Public buildings

The heart of any Roman town was the *forum*, a sort of civic centre, and Caistor St Edmund was no exception to the rule.

Work on the construction of a *forum* began in the middle of the 2nd century, and it was laid out according to a plan which was fairly standard to all small towns in Britain at this time.

The most important part was the *basilica*, a long open hall with the roof supported on arches running the full length of the building, and with a small room projecting at each end. In the centre and projecting to one side was the *curia*, in which the *ordo* met to discuss and decide on matters relating to the administration of the town and the countryside within the area of its jurisdiction. The small rooms at each end were offices for town officials and for the magistrates who dispensed justice and settled disputes. The great hall itself was used for public events, the people having the right to attend meetings to discuss decisions reached by the *ordo*.

The *basilica* was built of mortared flint with stringcourses - layers of bricks laid horizontally to tie the flint together. It was roofed in tiles and may have been one of the few buildings in town at this time to be constructed entirely of stone. The main door led to a flight of steps giving access down to a paved courtyard in the middle of the forum which served as a market place and for open air public ceremonies.

Thus the *basilica* formed one side of the *forum*, the other three being made up of long ranges of offices and shops with entrances into the forum from the outside, directly opposite the entrance to the basilica. At least some of the shops and offices were built on flint foundations, but superstructures generally consisted of unfired clay brick, rather like the clay lump used in Norfolk farm buildings until quite recently.

The *forum* was served by drains - deep trenches lined by timber and probably covered by wooden planks - which led to a large soakaway in one corner. The outside wall of the *forum* may have been decorated with stone columns, but if so these were only at either side of the main entrance.

The first *forum* was destroyed by fire, probably accidentally, in or about AD 200. The remains of the burnt out shell were demolished. The site then lay derelict for almost a century before a new *forum* was built about AD 300.

How the town was served by and housed its local government we have no idea, but during this long intervening period there was no *forum* or *basilica* to act a civic centre. When the *forum* was rebuilt it was on a much smaller scale, about two-thirds the size of the original, and it was built on top of a platform formed by the demolished remains of its predecessor. This meant the second *forum* was subsequently covered only by a shallow layer of topsoil, and it has been badly disturbed by ploughing since the end of the Roman period. In contrast, the remains of the first *forum* were to an extent preserved by the rubble which covered them.

The second *forum* was not only smaller than the first; it was also much simpler in form, with fewer rooms for shops and offices. Also, some of the rooms seem to have been lived in, something not normally expected in so important a building. The site of the *basilica* is not known. If there was one it may have been completely destroyed by the plough.

This later destruction also means we have no idea how long the second *forum* stayed in use, but it may have remained as a place of business and justice until the end of the 4th century. Its greatly reduced size, compared with the earlier version, may be another reflection of a decrease in the importance and richness of the town in its later years.

Public baths, essential to any Roman community for hygiene and as a social club, stood in the western sector of the town. Because later plough damage was severe little is known about them, but they do seem to have been built between about AD 180 and AD 200. Again, it is not known how long they remained in use. They seem to have been of the normal Turkish (more accurately called Roman) bath system, with a series of rooms going from cold to extremely hot, a small swimming pool, changing rooms and an open courtyard for games and exercises.

Being just inside the walls, but close to the river Tas, the baths could have been supplied with water quite easily. Foul water drained back into the river. Houses and workshops also needed a regular supply, and although excavations have produced no evidence to support the idea there must have been a system of pipes, possibly of lead but more likely of hollow wooden logs joined together with iron collars. Water was pumped into the system at some suitable source outside the town, perhaps higher up the river or on the other side of the town at one of the springs which feed several small streams running down into the Tas.

Roman Caistor was defended by a flint wall standing some 12ft high in front of a great earthen rampart with a deep ditch dug outside it. The wall and rampart were breached by four gates, one in the middle of each side, with the main streets of the town running through them, flanked on each side by a stone tower.

To the north and south the ditches were continuous across the front of the gates, suggesting there must have been bridges, probably of wood, to allow traffic through. On the east side the ditches were crossed by a causeway with a road on top, while to the west there was no ditch at all. Instead, the wet valley of the Tas took its place. Attached to the outer face of the wall were a number of small towers, or bastions, which allowed defenders a clear sight of any attacker.

There is no detailed evidence of when the defences were erected, but a date in the 4th century seems probable. The area defended represents only about half of that originally laid out in streets. Again, it is an indication of the decline of the town in its later stages.

Town walls in the Roman empire were sometimes held to be a mark of prestige and importance. At Caistor they must also have given some measure of security to the inhabitants against the threat of ravening Saxon raiders who by the 4th century were beginning to threaten the east coast.

Within the walled area stood two temples, small stone towers with lean-to roofs covering walkways around them. A third similar temple stood outside of the town about a quarter of a mile to the north east. This stood in its own walled enclosure, and although the building itself is probably of the 4th century large numbers of earlier coins have been found on the site. It is possible, therefore, there is an earlier temple underneath the later one. Houses and workshops stood around the outside of the walled area, although not so closely packed as those inside the walls.

The largest of the suburbs was on the east along both sides of the main road leading out of the main gate. Here there were bronze workshops producing, among other things, plain safety-pin type brooches. One of the town's cemeteries may also have been in this area.

To the west, on the other side of the Tas, where two or three Roman roads came together to cross the river, there must have been a bridge or some sort of crossing place. Again, the west bank of the river was lined with buildings, including workshops and storehouses. There may have been another cemetery here too, perhaps on a low hill overlooking the town.

At its height Caistor's population could have run into several thousand.

Many more people in the surrounding countryside would have used the town regularly for shopping and business. A modern comparison in population terms would be a large village, perhaps something like Hingham.

The rural network

Caistor stood at the centre of a web of roads which reached out to all parts of the county.

The main route connecting it to the south of England was the Pye Road, the modern A140, which ran to the city of Colchester. In Norfolk there were two settlements along this road, a straggle of houses at Long Stratton and a small town at Scole where the road crossed the river Waveney.

Running west from Caistor was the main road connecting Norfolk with the Midlands. It has been properly defined in recent years from aerial photographs and from fieldwork. It ran through Ketteringham and Crownthorpe - where there was a small roadside settlement and a temple - and on along the present line of Watton High Street through a small Roman British town at Threxton. From here it crossed the sandy wastes of Breckland and moved on towards Denver and the fens.

At Denver it was joined by a second east-west road which ran through Crimplesham, Stradsett and Fincham - where there may have been a wayside village - crossing the Peddars Way near Castle Acre at an unlocated crossroads. This road then continued through the northern part of central Norfolk with settlements along its line at Kempstone, Billingford and Brampton. It reached the river Bure at Wayford Bridge and may have swung south across the Isle of Flegg towards Caister on Sea.

After these two roads had joined at Denver they plunged across the fens heading towards the Roman town of Durobrivae (Water Newton, near Peterborough). This portion of the route subsequently became known as the Fen Causeway.

Other roads crossing this system connected settlements one to another. One example is a side road from Kempstone which ran to the Romano British village at Toftrees, near Fakenham, and then on to the coast near Holkham.

There must have been dozens more undiscovered side roads. Many were built of flint and gravel metalling, which proved unusually attractive to later medieval builders and farmers for re-use in other jobs. Thus many original surfaces have long since vanished. Sometimes all that remains are the ditches which acted as drains down either side of the road. In

Roman bath-house similar to that found at Brampton. The temperature inside would fall from very hot at the end nearest the stoke house to bracing in the cold plunge bath at the other end.

other places nothing remains but the alignment of the road preserved as an old track, hedge line or parish boundary.

Where roads had to cross wet land such as river valleys, or the great expanse of the fens, they were carried on corduroy timber causeways which are sometimes preserved by the waterlogged ground in which they were laid. A nice example of this was excavated at Brampton in the 1970s.

More information about Roman roads can be found in No 2 of the Norfolk Origins series, "Roads and Tracks."

If Caistor was the Roman equivalent of Norwich then small towns like Brampton and Threxton correspond to the modern market towns of Swaffham and Aylsham.

Best known of these is Brampton which has been excavated over several years by Keith and Vivienne Knowles. The town itself was about a fifth the size of Caistor, yet it was surrounded by a deep ditch. No evidence has been found of a rampart or stone wall.

The only known building of any substantial proportion inside the town was a small bath house which was almost entirely robbed of its stone in recent centuries. However, the town also contained a series of small houses and workshops built of timber on flint foundations and used for various sorts of metalworking. Although it lay close to the river Bure there were several wells dug into the natural clay and lined with planks. The wells would have served the houses and workshops.

But the most interesting part of Roman Brampton lies outside the ditched area, along both sides of the main road which comes in from the west. Here, in a sort of industrial suburb, remains have been found of almost 200 pottery kilns, great clay lined furnaces dug into the ground and fired with wood, in which a large range of different sorts of pottery vessels were made.

Some of these, coarse grey utilitarian vessels like pots and pans, were made mostly for sale to local inhabitants, although some were traded up to 30 or 40 miles from the town. Some of the kilns were also used specifically for the manufacture of the flagons (pottery wine bottles) and

Roman pots for food preparation and storage - these types were all made in the pottery kilns at Brampton.

Romano British pottery kiln, of the type used at Brampton. The dome is partly cut away to show the internal workings. Meanwhile the potter fills in a crack which has developed as the kiln heats up.

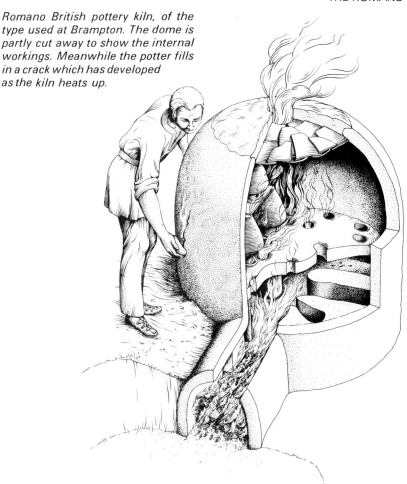

mortaria (pottery mixing bowls) found in every Romano British kitchen.

These more specialist pots were made for the local market and for export. Some of them, which had the name of the potter or pottery firm which made them stamped on the rim (Aesuminus, for example) were shipped out of Brampton, probably down the Bure, and carried to the north of Britain by sea. In any event they have been found as far afield as a Roman fort on the Antonine Wall near Edinburgh.

The town may not have been deliberately sited for the pottery industry. It may have grown from a series of houses and shops near a Roman fort positioned to guard the crossing of the Roman road over the river Bure. To the south of Brampton the Roman road has a peculiar dog-leg, and the fort may have been situated there, though this is pure guesswork. When the troops were withdrawn a few years after the Boudiccan revolt the houses and buildings which had provided goods and services for the army would have turned into a civilian town.

Given good communications provided by the river and the road it soon became a flourishing market centre. With the availability of quality clay, which was still being used for making bricks in the 19th century, it is no surprise a pottery industry grew there, probably around AD 100.

On the southern border of the county a Roman town grew up at Scole where the Pye Road crossed the river Waveney on the site of the modern A140 bridge. It was also crossed by an east-west road running along the north side of the Waveney valley.

Somewhere in this part of the Iceni territory was a settlement called Villa Faustini, and Scole is a good contender for the title. It does have its rivals, though.

Unlike Brampton, Scole was not, as far as we know, surrounded by a defensive ditch but was a ribbon development along the Pye and the east-west roads, with houses in little side streets filling the angles between them. There has been some excavation in the last 20 years, but most of the Roman settlement is now buried under the housing estates around the edge of Scole village.

Of the other roadside settlements we know much less, and usually only what can be gleaned from the evidence of pottery, building material and metal objects found on the surface of the land. Some, like Threxton and Brettenham, seem to have been centred on spots where a road, in this case the Peddars Way, crossed a river. They seem to have been farming settlements, perhaps with markets where local produce was bought and sold. Others, like Kempstone, where the surrounding fields are covered with iron slag, probably had more of an industrial economy.

There may have been a dozen or so communities like these in Norfolk, each with a population of hundreds or even thousands. The majority of the population, however, lived on the land outside of these nucleated settlements.

Country houses

All over the province were country houses which any Roman citizen would recognise, no matter what part of the empire he came from. There was an element of standardisation about many of them.

These were the buildings we now call villas, and although in Latin the word described almost any type of house it is now used for one particular sort of building. These are the Roman-style houses at the centre of large farms or country estates inhabited by retired civil servants who had come to Britain from other provinces to serve in the local administration, or by wealthy local people who had acquired a taste for the Roman way of life.

The classic Roman villa was a large stone building roughly the equivalent of a small stately home or well-to-do country house of the 18th or 19th centuries. It is not always easy to recognise them in East Anglia. In other parts of Britain these villas can be detected on hundreds of sites because of the huge amounts of building stone around in the fields. In Norfolk, of course, Romano British farmers did not have access to large amounts of stone. Instead, many of the farms were built out of timber, rather like the rich houses of the Middle Ages.

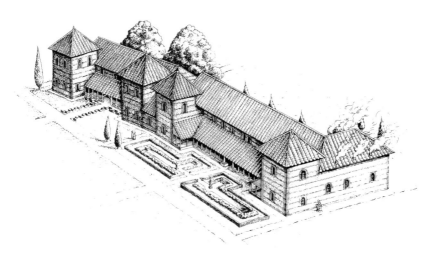

The Roman villa at Gayton Thorpe, as it may have looked in its heyday. The Norfolk villas are generally less elaborate than those in the South of England; Gayton Thorpe villa is two linked buildings. The map on pages 72-73 indicates the known villa sites mentioned in the text.

They were comfortable and often well appointed, but the materials have not survived as well as stone would have done. Only in the western part of Norfolk were chalk, flint and carrstone which could be found locally, and Barnack stone, brought in from the other side of the fens, used on a large scale.

Here in the west was a string of villas running from south to north along the western slope of the massive chalk ridge which forms the backbone of this part of the landscape. They were actually positioned along the Icknield Way which, although it had its origins in prehistory, continued to be used throughout the Roman period.

From Narborough in the south through Gayton, Gayton Thorpe, Grimston, Congham, Appleton, West Newton, Snettisham, Heacham and Hunstanton the villas were strung out every few miles along the road. In other parts of Norfolk villa sites are known at places like Tivetshall St Margaret, but nowhere else are they so tightly packed as in the west.

Norfolk villas, generally speaking, are smaller and less elaborate than those in the south of England, but they still display every aspiration to the Roman way of life.

Many of them were fronted by a colonnaded porch with a row of rooms behind. In the centre was a large dining room, called the *triclinium*, which normally had a fancy mosaic floor and was the main reception room for greeting and entertaining guests. The other rooms had private apartments for the family often with a bath suite at one end. This was served by a hypocaust to heat both air and water. Similar hypocausts were to be found in some living rooms. At Gayton Thorpe, the best known of Norfolk's Roman villas since it was excavated by Donald Atkinson in 1928, there are actually two buildings of very similar plan side-by-side joined by a small linking room. One of the buildings had a bath suite and central dining room while the other, though not so well preserved, seems not to have been so luxurious.

It is a puzzle why two separate buildings were linked in this way. If it was simply a case of increasing the size of the original building, then why did not the owner build on a large wing? Perhaps we see the result of a family split.

No villa buildings are visible now, of course. Indeed, all that remains is a few scattered patches of building material, usually fragments of red roof tile, and occasionally tesserae from mosiac floors, or pieces of wall plaster which adorned the inside of many of the rooms and was often painted with simple coloured stripes or more elaborate patterns - the Roman version of wallpaper!

The Gayton Thorpe villa has also turned up one pretty little problem. Among the tiles found on the side was one stamped EG VI VIC. This is part of the name LEGIO VI VICTRIX, the Latin title of the 6th Legion, which from the second century onwards was stationed at York.

It is known the army made bricks and tiles which it used for building its forts. But these were all made on the spot. Consequently, the only place where tiles of the 6th Legion would be expected to turn up is York. What is the tile doing nearly 200 miles away at Gayton Thorpe? It seems unlikely that a load of army surplus tiles was shipped to Norfolk. Perhaps a legion veteran bought his retirement home in Norfolk and brought a piece of tile with him as a keepsake.

Farm and field

The villa buildings were really no more than fancy farm houses. In fact most of the countryside was divided into large estates, or small farms, which produced food for their own use. Any surplus was used to pay the Imperial taxes or sold for profit.

Those estates which had villas similar to Gayton Thorpe probably farmed areas of many thousands of acres, or areas as large as a modern parishes. There were also small farms, such as the one known from air photographs at Hassingham, near Cantley, on the edge of the estuary - which had perhaps 50 acres at the most, and wooden huts instead of farm houses.

Again, the largest estates seem to have been in the west of the county, and it is likely they took advantage of the west slope of the chalk ridge from which a number of springs debouched. In any event the villas were built at the level of the springs. It meant the estates always had a source of water to serve the house and for the cattle and sheep.

The springs also turned into wandering rivers which cut small valleys into the side of the chalk, which meant the estates had a large number of types of soil and a variety of resources available.

A farm like Gayton, for example, would have been able to graze sheep on the chalk ridge a couple of miles to the east, and cattle in the river valley, near the villa, running off to the west. On the sides of the chalk ridge some of the soil was admirably suited for growing cereal crops. Other soils could have supported woodland suitable for pigs and coppice to supply timber for fences and buildings.

A large villa estate probably employed several hundred people living almost as slaves in hamlets and villages scattered around the farm, and with no freedom to move elsewhere. Small farms, on the other hand, seem to have been run by owner-families with no outside help at all.

Most of the crops are still familiar today. Wheat and barley were the commonest grains, with rye and oats grown in small quantities. Root crops like turnips and mangolds are said by Roman historians to have been grown to feed livestock. Herds of cattle and flocks of sheep and pigs were reared where possible, but there was a continuous problem in finding sufficient grazing to see large flocks through the winter.

Roots were fed to some animals kept in byres, and hay was also harvested and kept for the winter. But there would not have been enough fodder for all the stock. There must have been a busy slaughtering period in the autumn when part of the flock was killed and the meat preserved for the winter by salting and smoking.

Grain was stored from one harvest to the next in jars, probably large storage vessels up to four or five feet high. Even so there must have been

The remains of a Roman landscape, buried under the modern one at Hopton with the modern A12 running through the middle of the picture. Dark cropmarks show where ditches once ran, marking out the boundaries of Romano British farm and fields, linked together by double-ditched trackways. (Photo: University of Cambridge, Committee for Aerial Photography.)

occasions when the British summer was so wet the crops had to be harvested before they were properly dry. It is easy to forget, given modern crop driers, that during the last few centuries corn crops were often gathered in October and November because the autumn was too wet to allow a proper harvest.

Every now and again stone or clay ovens are found on Roman farm sites, and archaeologists invariably refer to them as corn driers. Since these are often no more than four or five feet long, however, they would not have allowed the whole of a crop to be dried out if it had been harvested wet.

It is more likely these "ovens" are malting kilns where barley was processed for brewing. The grain was soaked in pits or jars of water until it began to sprout, and then roasted on the hot floor of a kiln to produce barley malt. These days we tend to think of malt mainly as an ingredient of beer, but it is actually a very good way of preserving grain and increasing its nutritional value. Malt can be used in baking and other forms of cooking as well as for producing beer.

There is no evidence for malt before the Roman period, and it is probably an invention brought to Britain at this time.

Crops and animals had not changed much from the Iron Age, but the subject is difficult to study. All that remain are bones and burnt seed. Certainly Roman farming was much more intensive than that of the Iron Age, and farming practices such as rotation, manuring and the use of nitrogen-fixing crops like peas and vetch would have been part of a system designed to make profit out of the land.

Produce from farms and smallholdings was used, first, to support those reliant on the land, and second, for taxes which for much of the Roman period were paid in kind rather than in cash. Each farm was given a quota, a certain amount of grain or animals, which were collected at local centres like the county town at Caistor, and shipped out to feed the armies garrisoning frontiers such as Hadrian's Wall. Any further surplus was sold either to neighbours or in the local market towns such as Brampton. Those who worked in industry probably relied on these markets for their supply of food.

This raises a particular problem. Among the villas along the Icknield Way there is no market town. Narford is perhaps the most likely candidate, although from what is known of this site it does not seem large enough. Also, the distance from the furthermost villas around Snettisham and Heacham is such that carriers would have had to travel for several days in order to transport produce to a market at Narford.

How these estates disposed of their surpluses is a puzzle. Perhaps it was done as a series of private deals between one landowner and another, rather as deals are struck in the back rooms of pubs to this day.

Food plants cultivated in the Iron Age and in the Roman period. Some of these survive today only as weeds.

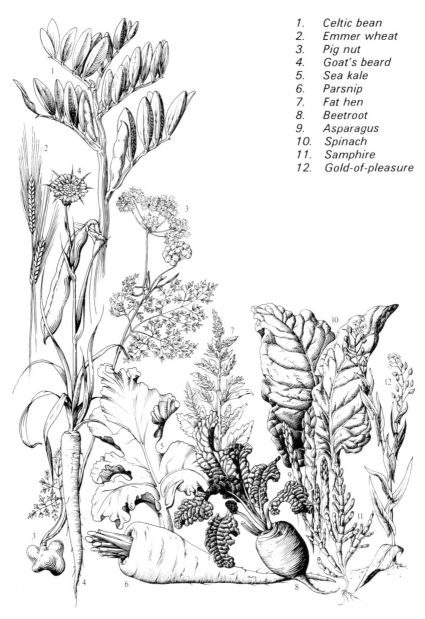

1. Celtic bean
2. Emmer wheat
3. Pig nut
4. Goat's beard
5. Sea kale
6. Parsnip
7. Fat hen
8. Beetroot
9. Asparagus
10. Spinach
11. Samphire
12. Gold-of-pleasure

Students taking the opportunity to view the foundations of the Roman barn at Weeting, when the site was clear after excavation.
(Photo: Poppyland Photos.)

The new lands

During the Iron Age the fens from Ely to Wisbech were a vast expanse of wet black peat in the south and tidal saltwater lagoons in the north. As the sea level dropped during the 1st century AD so the northern part of the fen began to dry, leaving huge expanses of land which belonged to no-one.

As far as Norfolk is concerned this is the stretch of land running from Upwell to West Walton near Wisbech, an area of many thousands of acres.

Once the salt had come out of the soil the land was very fertile indeed. Even the salt water which still flowed up the river beds at high tide provided a useful source of income.

Since this was new land with no previous owner it became the personal property of the emperor. Thus an Imperial estate was established running from Denver, on the Norfolk edge of the fen, through to Spalding, and further north almost as far as Lincoln.

This vast expanse was administered for Hadrian and his successors by procurators who had their headquarters at Stonea, near March in Cambridgeshire, once one of the strongholds of the Iceni. Here, around AD 120, a large stone tower was built only a few hundred yards from the former Iceni site.

Now the fens were being tamed. Vast profits flowed into the Imperial coffers, channelled through the Stonea offices. Estate farming here was very specialised because there was always a risk of salt water flooding the fields during the spring tides. There may have been very little arable land. Certainly large flocks of sheep grazed over small fields between roadways and watercourses, and it is noticeable that when large numbers of bones are found on fenland sites older sheep are much more common than young sheep. This suggests they were kept for milk and wool rather than for meat.

In this connection it is interesting that during the later Roman period there was an Imperial monopoly on weaving. The wool from fenland sheep presumably went to Imperial weaving sheds or was shipped out along the network of fen roads.

The other main product was salt, which was needed for preserving meat and fish, for treating hides, and for feeding to animals in other parts of the area.

Every high tide the water flooded up a network of natural streams and creeks which ran several miles into the estate. It was then directed into a series of artificial ditches and tanks where it was allowed to settle, and ladled into pottery troughs set up over peat fires. The water evaporated, leaving salt crystals behind.

People doing this sort of work probably saw little profit. Indeed, it is striking that whenever fenland sites are dug very few luxury items are found, and almost no metalwork. Coins are very rare indeed. The Imperial estate may have supplied all the workers' needs so they did not require, or had no opportunity to earn, money.

Roman salt-making at Denver, on the edge of the Fens. Salt water has been evaporating for some time in the oblong tank, and the concentrated brine is now being ladled into clay troughs for final boiling.

The biggest threat to the fens came not from the sea but from water in the rivers running out from the Midlands. Nowadays the Witham, Nene and the Ouse run through channels between high artificial banks which contain and control the water and prevent major floods. In the Roman period these same rivers were wild and flowed through great meandering channels, often changing their courses by breaking out with catastrophic effect.

The authorities tried to reduce this risk by building a huge catchwater drain across the peat fen from between Ely and Cambridge up into Lincolnshire. This is called the Car Dyke, traditionally regarded as a Roman canal. However, it is not continuous, and in several place there are large causeways which would have prevented the movement of ships. It is more likely this dyke was intended to divert some of the water from the rivers and spread it out across the fen, thus reducing the risk.

It appears to have worked well for the first couple of centuries. Then in the late 3rd and 4th centuries AD the climate deteriorated and became wetter. The dykes were no longer able to cope with the increased flow of water, and many sites of this period show evidence of freshwater flooding. Instead, new settlements were established on top of the flood silts.

By the 4th century it seems there were fewer but larger sites in the fens. It is even possible the Imperial estate was "de-nationalised" and sold to private landowners.

The new Britons

It is easy to think of the people of Norfolk at this time as Romans, but this is not accurate. The vast majority were the descendants of the Iron Age tribes which had populated the country before the conquest. The invasion did introduce some foreigners, largely in the ranks of the army, but again, relatively few of these were Romans from Italy. The army ranks tended to be full of the citizens of Roman provinces including Africa, Syria, Spain, Germany and Gaul.

Some of the officers, civil servants, generals and governors may have been Romans, but many were also provincials.

The people who lived off the land had no foreign blood in them at all. Indeed and despite an increasingly Roman way of life, they may still have thought of themselves as Iceni.

It is difficult to calculate the size of the population. Even if all the Norfolk sites were known, and the number of people who lived in each one, it would still be impossible to tell if they were all inhabited at precisely the same time. All we can do is assume a relatively small number of people in the towns with the majority in closely spaced farms all over the county, and a total mounting to several hundred thousand.

The landscape and the population, in fact, may have been very little different to Norfolk in the Middle Ages.

One way in which Roman customs were absorbed was the language spoken at different levels of society. Ordinary folk probably carried on with the language spoken in the Iron Age, a Celtic tongue similar to modern Welsh mingled with a few Latin words. This is most obvious in personal names. Potters who occasionally signed their names on vessels sometimes gave away the fact that they had Latin and Iron Age names in use together.

In other parts of England some Celtic names have survived, particularly the names of rivers. Avon is an example. In East Anglia the effect of the subsequent Saxon invasion was so devastating that all trace of the Celtic language seems to have been swept away.

At a higher level of society Latin was in greater use. One Greek name has turned up in Norfolk, too, at Gayton Thorpe, where a potsherd bearing the name Odysseus (in Greek letters) suggests that a Greek slave may have kept his old name. It is a very rare example, however.

The language of the few Romans who did come to Britain was Latin and it is assumed it became the language of administration, the language in which central records were kept, and the language of the Romano-British law courts.

It was a Roman tradition, of course, to impose the legal system of Rome on all its provinces, and although there is no specific evidence it can be assumed that in Norfolk criminal cases and civil disputes were settled in courts probably in the basilica at Caistor and that these cases were heard and disputed in Latin.

The modern legal system still carries traces of Roman laws. Many Latin phrase like *"habeas corpus"* are still in use.

Writing was not uncommon, but records and documents were kept on parchment and tablets of wax in wooden frames, and survivals are rare. None have come down to us in Norfolk. From time to time words or letters are found scratched on pieces of pottery, and one nice example is a pot base from Scole which displays a rather bad alphabet. It looks like the result of a schoolboy writing exercise.

The Romano British at home

The Roman way of life was felt particularly strongly in the home life of the middle and upper classes and most evidently among those who could afford stone buildings such as villas. Stone was not used for housing during the Iron Age. The method was a Roman introduction. All that could be found locally, however, was flint and carrstone, and these were used as rubble held together with hard lime mortar and rows of flat bricks, or stringcourses. The walls were often faced with knapped flint to give a smooth and agreeable surface, and the inside of the walls covered with a layer of plaster which was painted for decoration.

Even in wooden buildings new fashions appeared. They tended to be built in the same shape as stone buildings, and were no longer round. The spaces between the timbers were filled with wattle and daub - woven branches or withies, plastered over with mud, straw and animal dung -which could be made far more attractive than it sounds.

The surface of the daub was often decorated with patterns pressed on with large rollers while the daub was still wet. The effect was something like the pargetted plastering still common in Suffolk and Essex. Wattle and daub was used as a building material until well into this century.

These new building fashions also brought a need for new industries, and lime kilns were established in the countryside to produce lime from chalk for making mortar and plaster. Other kilns made bricks and tiles. Some buildings had floors of red brick tiles, particularly those which had hypocaust or central heating systems, yet another Roman introduction.

A space was dug under the floor with a flue leading in from the outside of the building. A fire, probably fuelled by wood, burned in the flue so that hot air circulated in the space under the floor. A floor of flagstones or tiles was supported on blocks of ground left unexcavated or on pillars of bricks mortared one on top of the other. The hot air then passed up through walls which incorporated flue tiles - square sectioned clay pipes like shoeboxes with the ends knocked out. These were mounted vertically so that the heat moved upwards, warmed the wall, and finally disappeared through vents in the roof.

Hypocausts of this sort were used to heat living rooms and bathrooms which were part and parcel of all the most comfortable Romano British homes. It must have been a very efficient system. With so much brick in use the floor and walls would have held the heat and acted like a giant night storage heater.

What portion of the population enjoyed such amenities is uncertain. The luxury buildings were substantially built, of course, and have survived in part. Less substantial buildings have disappeared completely.

The houses of the ordinary people, and many of the houses in small towns and villages, were built of timber and clay. All that survives of one building at Scole, for example, is a rectangular floor of gravel with a few post sockets around the edge. It must have had walls but these may have rested directly on the ground surface with no foundations. The roof may have been of thatch.

It sounds like a poor hovel but there is no reason why it was not comfortable and perfectly weatherproof. Timbers laid directly on to the

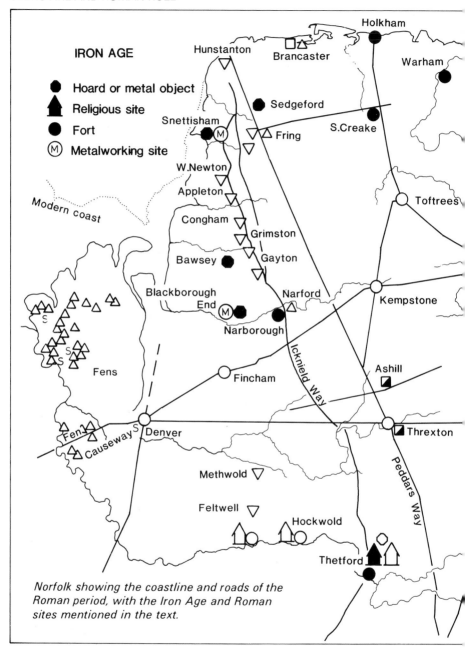

Norfolk showing the coastline and roads of the Roman period, with the Iron Age and Roman sites mentioned in the text.

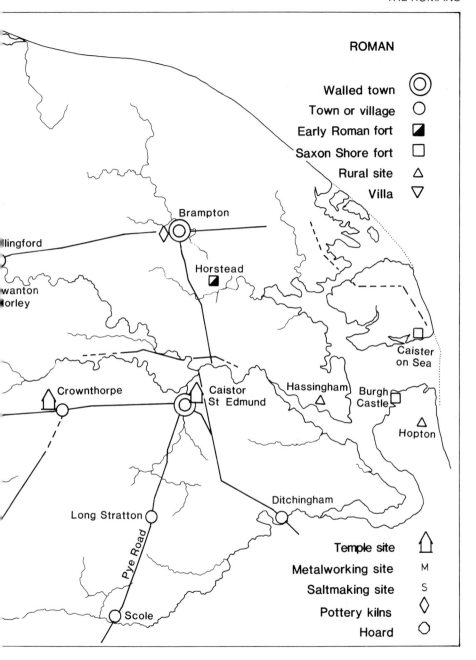

ROMAN

Walled town	◎
Town or village	○
Early Roman fort	◪
Saxon Shore fort	□
Rural site	△
Villa	▽

Brampton

llingford

Horstead

wanton
orley

Caister
on Sea

Crownthorpe

Caistor
St Edmund

Hassingham

Burgh
Castle

△
Hopton

Ditchingham

Long Stratton

Pye Road

Temple site	⌂
Metalworking site	M
Saltmaking site	S
Pottery kilns	◇
Hoard	⬡

Scole

ground with uprights joined on in fact form a very firm framework for a building. Many Norfolk barns built this way 300 or 400 years ago are still in use today.

Food and dress

No Romano British clothes have survived in Norfolk. Occasional scraps of cloth have turned up, usually in waterlogged deposits where the conditions were too wet for the normal processes of decay, but none of these was big enough to reconstruct clothing. Leather has fared better and several sandals have survived, ranging from soft delicate items like ballet shoes to more durable hobnailed open-toed work boots.

Representations on locally cut gems set in finger rings show people dressed in the classic manner - men in short tunics, or togas, and women in flowing ankle length dresses - but these are always formal poses and may not accurately represent what people wore during their workaday lives.

Jewellery and clothes fastenings made of metal have survived better. In the 1st and 2nd centuries AD bronze brooches, probably used as cloak or tunic fasteners, were very popular indeed. In the latter part of the Roman period they hardly appear at all, suggesting either that clothes were fastened with perishable materials such as wooden buttons or that garments were put on over the head with no side openings.

Food and eating habits were strongly influenced by Roman ideas. Dining room furniture appears in Britain, probably for the first time, and the Roman habit of reclining on couches and eating from low tables was probably practised.

Knives and forks do not seem to have been used at table, but spoons made of bronze or silver certainly were. Large numbers of cups and plates of pottery, pewter, bronze and silver, and glass, were available to the different classes, made either locally or imported from abroad.

Roman recipes were presumably adopted. The most important kitchen utensil was the *mortarium*, a large pottery dish with an inside surface studded with small sharp stones. It was used as a sort of food processor. Basic ingredients were ground into a thick stock, or gruel, which was cooked in pottery or metal vessels on an iron grid over an open fire of charcoal.

Most of these ingredients were already available in Britain - grains such as wheat, barley and oats, and meat from cows, sheep, pigs and goats. From time to time the bones of other animals are found during excavations showing obvious butchery marks. It seems the Romano British were quite prepared to eat almost anything on four legs, including horses, dogs and cats.

Fish was certainly eaten, but fishbones are difficult to find on excavated sites. There is plenty of evidence, however, for domestic chickens and wild birds, including sometimes pigeon.

Exotic foods were imported, and the growing prosperity of Romano Britain opened up rich new markets for traders. At the ports around the coast evidence for the import of fruit such as figs and peaches, and spices including coriander, has been found.

There is a tradition that the Romans were also responsible for the introduction of rabbits, pheasants and fallow deer into Britain. If so, they were certainly intended for food.

Vegetables were eaten, too. Some, like broad beans and radishes are still grow today, but others have fallen out of fashion over the years and are only found as wild plants today. Pig-nuts and goat's-beard are two examples.

The Roman proclivity for oysters is legendary. Sometimes sites can be recognised simply from quantities of oyster shells lying around on the surface of fields. In the days before industrial pollution the oyster beds of southern and eastern England must have produced thousands of tons a year. British oysters were often mentioned by Roman writers as a particular delicacy.

Freshwater shellfish, including the freshwater mussel, were certainly eaten. In fact these molluscs also produce pearls. One Roman historian claimed that Julius Caesar's main aim in coming to Britain was to make profit from the exploitation of British pearl mussels.

The most common import of all was wine, a trade established long before the conquest. During the early part of the Roman period Italian and French wines were imported, in amphorae, but as these do not appear in later centuries it is possible a change was made to German wines in barrels.

Other commodities in amphorae included olive oil and *garum* - a sort of fermented sauce of rotten fish - mostly from the coasts of Spain and Portugal.

However, there is no reason to suppose that any of these imports put an end to the traditional British enthusiasm for brewing.

Religious give and take

Unlike the later British empire, Rome did not insist on converting subjects to its own religions. Indeed, at the time of the conquest Roman religion was already a mix of traditional Italian gods and those of many other countries, including Greece and Egypt. Soldiers from the provinces brought many of their own gods with them and these, with the Roman gods, were thrown into a melting pot with the Celtic deities of Iron Age Britain.

Not surprisingly, perhaps, in the Romano British temples a single god was often given two names, one Roman and the other native. Thus the Roman god Mars is sometimes linked with the Celtic god Lenus; and the Roman goddess Minerva - herself a mix of the Roman original and the Greek Athene - identified with the Celtic goddess Sul, patroness of the hot water springs at Bath (Sul-Minerva).

In this way the Romans managed to introduce their own religions without offending local sensitivities. The system seems to have worked.

Even towards the end of the Roman period the native Celtic gods were still being worshipped. Indeed, there is evidence from other parts of the province that invading armies often worshipped in native shrines alongside the conquered people. Along Hadrian's Wall it is common to find stone altars dedicated by soldiers to local gods or goddesses. So, although the Druids had supposedly been wiped out in AD 61 the religion they served still survived.

Reconstruction of a late Roman (Roman-Celtic) temple, with a tall central tower (the cella), surrounded by a portico.

One way in which Roman influence can be detected is in the introduction of an entirely new cult, the worship of the spirit, the Genius, of the dead emperors. The most famous example is the cult of the deified Claudius whose temple at Colchester was destroyed by Boudicca's rebels. The remains survive as the vaults of Colchester castle.

Here there was a huge temple with stone columns around a central shrine, or *cella*, in which stood a statue of the emperor. Local people, officials and dignitaries were expected to take oaths of loyalty, burn incense and make offerings. Similar temples presumably existed in other towns.

Temples of local gods and Roman equivalents were often small, simple buildings ten or 20ft square consisting of a central shrine with a colonnaded walk around the outside.

In these Romano British temples it is assumed the worshippers walked or even danced round the outer porch and threw their offerings to the gods through the doors or windows of the cella. When such sites are excavated, as at Hockwold-cum-Wilton and Caistor St Edmund, large numbers of coins are often found. The offerings sometimes took the form of small statues of the gods or of birds or animals. Occasionally there were inscriptions made out of bronze letters nailed to the walls of the temples.

Perhaps the priest who ran the temple sold nicknacks of this sort to worshippers who would then dedicate them in the temple. This would provide the temples with a regular source of income and is the pagan equivalent of candles in a Christian church.

Particular dedications might be made if a worshipper wanted to make a specific request of a god, and sometimes small bronze models of parts of the human body are found; eyes, hands, feet, to mention but three. They may have been dedicated by people who had something wrong with those particular organs and who were hoping for a divine cure.

The most colourful evidence of religious life comes in the form of small sheets of lead, tightly rolled and thrown on to the temple floors. If they can be successfully unrolled they are often found to contain scratched messages or curses which request the god to punish someone who has offended the worshipper in some way. They are often difficult to translate because they are written in a poor script, but they do record offences like adultery and the theft of a pig.

The best local example, concerning the theft of a towel, was found in river dredgings at Caistor St Edmund and probably originated from one of the temples. Presumably the contents of the temple were cleaned out at regular intervals, and in this case thrown into the river, to make room for the next batch of offerings.

The Celtic style of worship performed at more natural places such as springs and forest clearings also continued. On a Roman site at Ashill, for example, were three deep wells lined with timber and used in the normal way for drawing water. When no longer required, either because a new source of water had been found or because the water in them was foul, then they were filled ceremoniously.

A wide range of objects has been preserved, because the infill soil remained waterlogged for 1900 years. A mass of brushwood was dropped to the bottom on which was laid whole pots, many with long strings tied to the neck so they could be lowered without breaking. Other objects included knives, wicker baskets and the skeletons of dogs, which may have had a special significance to whichever deity was being worshipped.

Because of the waterlogging the brushwood, mainly hazel, was wonderfully preserved. The very lowest layer consisted of twigs with the flower buds still closed. In a succession of layers going higher up the fill of the well the development of the hazel could be seen, so that in the highest layer the flowers had been and gone. Instead, the twigs carried fully formed nuts. It appears, therefore, that the filling of the well took place throughout the spring and summer with a layer of brushwood and other offerings being deposited every two or three weeks.

This special reverence for wells is reminiscent of the supposedly Christian well dressing ceremonies which still take place in some Derbyshire villages.

The site of a Romano Celtic temple at Thetford yielded a spectacular collection of Roman gold and silver, perhaps the possessions of a temple, buried in the ground in order to protect them from some sort of danger in about AD 390.

This hoard, known as the Thetford Treasure and discovered in 1979, contained silver spoons — probably used in some sort of sacred meal - many bearing inscriptions such as *"Dei Fauni Blotugi"* (the property of the god Faunus/Blotugus). In all almost a dozen names associated with this hoard are equated with that of Faunus.

It is further evidence for the survival of the worship of Celtic gods.

With the spoons was a staggeringly rich collection of gold jewellery including necklaces, belt buckles, pendants and finger rings, all new and apparently unworn. They appear at first sight to be the stock-in-trade of a jeweller, but one of the rings has a central setting for a gem supported by two tiny bird figures, apparently woodpeckers.

The Latin for woodpecker is *picus*. Faunus, originally an Italian nature spirit, was the son of a god named Picus. This is surely too much of a coincidence, and it may be that all of the jewellery was bought or made to dedicate in the temple which was only about 100 metres from the great Icenian site of Gallows Hill, itself probably religious.

This is an example of a native site continuing in use right through the period of Roman rule.

The coming of Christianity

Christianity seems to have appeared in the province in the 2nd century AD. From time to time it was tolerated, but at other times followers of the cult were persecuted and martyred. This was not because the Roman authorities had any particular grudge against Christianity but rather because the Christians, unlike the adherents of most other religions in

Lead tank found somewhere near Oxborough. The cross-like motif in the circle might be a Christian symbol. If so, then the tank is almost certainly a baptismal font from a Romano British church.

the empire, refused to perform their civic duty and take vows in the temple of the spirit of the emperor.

When Christianity was officially accepted early in the 4th century AD, and in consequence took over much of the religious life of the empire, the Christians themselves launched a campaign of persecution against pagans far worse than anything they had suffered.

For one short period about AD 360 Rome was ruled by an emperor, Julian, who had little time for Christianity and who supported many pagan cults. This period saw the revival of many Romano British temples which had probably been closed down by the Christians. Julian's successors, however, reverted to Christian intolerance to such an extent that by the end of the 4th century the plight of the pagans must have been dire indeed.

This may be the reason the Thetford Treasure was buried, to preserve it from excessive Christian zeal.

Precise evidence for Christianity among the Iceni is hard to come by. However, in the great collection of silver plate found at Mildenhall in the 1940s, and known as the Mildenhall Treasure, there are three silver spoons inscribed with the Christogram, or chi-rho, a Christian symbol made up of the first two letter of Christ's name in Greek. This at least suggests they were used in Christian ritual.

The Imperial post

No empire can exist without efficient communications, and the empire of Rome was no exception. The framework was a little like the Wells Fargo Company of America. A series of couriers travelled along the great network of roads which spanned the empire carrying messages from Rome to the provincial capitals, county towns, and to the civil servants in the villages.

It is possible the roads were kept in good condition more for this purpose than anything else. Indeed, the way villages can sometimes be found along Roman roads at intervals of five to ten miles is a clear indication of how the system worked.

A courier carrying official despatches travelled in a light carriage pulled by one or two horses. At each village along the road was a *mansio,* or staging post at which the courier could eat, rest, and change the horses. A large number of Imperially owned horses were presumably kept for this purpose at each of the staging posts paid for, no doubt, by local taxes.

By this means a letter could be sent from Rome to London in a matter of days. A speed of 10 mph could be achieved without undue stress to the system.

Trade and markets

If the roads were primarily intended for official communications the local population must surely have taken advantage of them for the purpose of local trade.

Small towns along the roads provided market places at which inhabitants of the surrounding countryside sold their surpluses and bought goods, particularly luxury items, which they could not manufacture for themselves.

Road transport in ancient times was regarded as a slow and expensive necessity. Land transport was 25 times more expensive than transport by water. The difference was that horses or oxen hauling heavy wooden waggons, even over the finest paved roads, could not pull any great weight. The load, in any event, was limited to 1500 Roman pounds, and a speed of one or two miles an hour was probably normal.

Another problem was that a team of eight oxen ate more weight in fodder than it could actually pull in a day. Therefore, unless the goods carried were of greater value than the hay or grain fed to the animals, road transport was hopelessly uneconomic.

The use of oxen proved to be the main drawback. Only when horses became more common as draught animals in the late Middle Ages did large scale land transport become a realistic proposition.

Water transport

Water was by far the cheapest method of transportation, and most of the goods moved around Norfolk would have gone on shallow wooden river boats which sailed from the coastal ports up rivers like the Bure, Yare, Wensum, and on the other side of the county, the Ouse. In return, goods from manufacturing centres like Brampton were shipped down river to be loaded on to seagoing vessels and distributed to other parts of the province, or overseas.

Small ports dotted the coastline. The best known was at Caister on Sea where seagoing craft hove-to in the shallows of what was then a great estuary but is now the marshes of the Bure. Merchants brought cargoes and sold them in the local markets.

No Roman ship survives in Norfolk, but evidence from the rest of the empire suggests that seagoing merchant vessels built of oak were propelled by a large single sail and steered by an oar.

River boats were in all probability very little different from Norfolk keels, predecessors of the wherry, which traded up the East Anglian rivers a couple of centuries ago.

A Roman cargo ship unloading at a riverside quay at Colchester. When Britain became a Roman province, trade with the Roman empire increased enormously. Britain became part of Europe's first common market. (Photo: Colchester and Essex Museum.)

The changing landscape

Today's Norfolk coastline is very different to that at the end of the Roman period.

The rivers to the east - the Yare, Bure and Waveney -still ran into the great estuary at Reedham, which left the area north of Yarmouth isolated as an island (the Isle of Flegg) in an expanse of tidal mudflats. The north end of the fens, flooded in the Iron Age, was now settled farmland left dry by falling sea levels. Norfolk's northern coastline was wild and sparsely populated.

Inland, the afforested area of the mid-Norfolk boulder clay was slowly being eaten away by farmers clearing ground. In fact much of the land cleared during the Roman period may well have reverted to forest again by the Middle Ages, when it was cleared once more.

Life in the boulder clay areas must have been as difficult as ever because although temperatures were slightly higher than might be expected today, the climate was also wetter.

The Saxon shore

The peace and quiet of Norfolk's Roman landscape first began to be disturbed about AD 200 when barbarian tribes from across the North Sea attacked the coastline. The problem was on a much bigger scale than this, however, for the whole of the northern frontier of the empire was threatened by the movements of Germanic and Mongoloid peoples pushing west and south.

Indeed, compared with that happened along the Rhine and Danube frontiers, Roman Britain seems to have escaped rather lightly.

Quite simply the Angles, Saxons and Frisians from northern Germany and Holland were themselves coming under pressure from tribes further east. Their response was to raid and infiltrate the rich Roman provinces along the English Channel. To the population of Norfolk it must have seemed a real emergency.

The Roman response was to develop a defensive framework within which the army and the fleet worked together to protect the coast. This entailed moving land forces from the north of England and southern Scotland, where they had been garrisoned throughout the 2nd century, and the building of garrison forts along the coast from Norfolk to Hampshire and Belgium to Normandy.

The new garrisons and their fleet detachments were put in the command of a new military supremo, the Count of the Saxon Shore.

The shore forts

The new garrisons had to be given strongpoints to defend, and a series of forts were built for this specific purpose. In the beginning there were two in Norfolk, one at Brancaster (Branodunum) on the north coast, and one at Caister on Sea (Roman name unknown) on the north side of the estuary.

Their layouts were little changed from those built during the previous two centuries. The main features were a square surrounded by a deep ditch, and stone wall with an earthen rampart behind. They also had the characteristic "playing card" corners of early rounded forts and a neat, orderly layout of buildings.

Today, nothing survives at Brancaster, but aerial photography and excavation have traced the original shape.

The discovery of two tiles stamped with the title lst Cohort of Aquitanians is evidence for the first garrison at Brancaster. At some point, perhaps in the late 3rd century, they were replaced by a cavalry regiment. This was Equites Dalmatae, originally raised in Dalmatia in northern Yugoslavia. The evidence for this garrison comes not from excavation but from the Notitia Dignitatum, a list compiled by the Imperial civil service of all official establishments in the empire.

Unlike Brancaster, the fort at Caister on Sea did not survive into the 4th century. It was replaced by another fort, built in what was then the most up-to-date military style, at Burgh Castle on the other side of the estuary.

Here, a massive wall of flint, held together with courses of red brick and faced with squared flints, was constructed with large circular towers attached to the outside of the walls. In the tops of these towers were large sockets which can still be seen today. There is controversy as to their purpose. They might have contained a central post which supported an umbrella-like roof. Or they may have been pivots for *ballistae*, giant crossbows which served the army during this period as artillery. They were capable of throwing iron tipped arrows eight or 10ft long over a distance of several hundred yards.

Inside the fort the stone buildings were laid out in a rather less regimented style than in the earlier forts. Indeed, the interior gives less of a military impression than, for example, Brancaster.

At any particular time, therefore, there were two Saxon shore forts in Norfolk, albeit a considerable distance apart. There might have been a third, perhaps near Cromer or Mundesley. But this part of the coast has eroded by several miles since the Roman period, and a third fort would have been destroyed by the sea.

83

Reconstruction of the iron cavalry helmet, found in the fort at Burgh Castle. The Normans were not the first to use nose-guards!

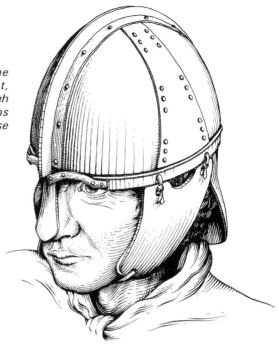

Between the forts, signal stations passed messages along the coast, warning the next fort in line of possible attack. On the north coast the isolated hillocks on the edge of the marshes, Gramborough Hill at Salthouse, Muckleburgh Hill at Kelling, and Warborough Hill at Stiffkey, all have Roman sites on top and probably supported beacons and semaphore stations.

These sites were also used in later times, particularly during the Napoleonic wars, and the common name Beacon Hill normally refers to this later use.

The end of the forts seems to have come peacefully. The disappearance of Brancaster, for example, was not due to enemy action but to abandonment and to the demolition of walls by medieval and later stone robbers who used the stones for churches and other buildings.

At Burgh Castle, Norfolk's best preserved Roman site, it is easy to see how this robbery took place. The casing is stripped off the walls to a height of eight to nine feet, as high as could conveniently be reached with a ladder. The nearby church in the village must surely have been built with this flint.

Final curtain

The end of the empire was dramatic.

The central authority of the emperor began to break down towards the end of the 4th century as the barbarian tribes Goths, Vandals and Huns, flooded over the borders. Garrisons from outlying provinces were recalled to Italy to fight a rearguard action, and by AD 410 most of the regular army units in Britain had gone.

In fact the ranks may have been depleted long before this. On several occasions Roman generals such as Magnus Maximus (in AD 383) and Constantine 111 (in AD 407) gathered armies and crossed from Britain to the Continent in vain attempts to win the Imperial throne for themselves. Their armies probably never returned to Britain, but were absorbed into what was left of the Roman army in France and Italy.

Because of these moves the degree of protection the Romano British population could expect from the Saxon raiders was very little indeed. Civil order and administration slowly broke down and the final withdrawal of the army, by the emperor Honorius in AD 410, was the last nail in the coffin of the province.

As Saxon raids gathered pace so the towns of Britain attempted to raise troops of their own. Some even hired groups of raiders as mercenaries to fight off the next batch of raiders. Alas, these measures merely delayed the inevitable.

By about AD 450 the Saxons were arriving in increasing numbers, not as raiders but as invaders. The native population, weakened by warfare, plague and famine, was unable to resist. Thus the newcomers were able to turn what had been Roman Norfolk into Anglo Saxon Norfolk.

The leaders changed. Now they were no longer Romano Britons speaking Latin but Saxon warriors with wooden shields and iron swords. The people were the same, however. They were the descendants of the Iceni tribesmen who had fought with Boudicca. Now they had to adapt to another way of life, another new language, and a new name.

Slowly, the grass grew over the remains of the old empire. In the years which followed the tumbled and dilapidated remains of Roman towns, forts, farms and villages became overgrown and deserted, the haunts of outlaws and wild beasts.

The pride which was Rome was gone forever.

The corner bastion and walls of the Roman fort of the Saxon Shore at Burgh Castle.

Warning

Reference to or representation of a site should not be taken as evidence that such a site may be visited. In almost every case sites are on private land. If permission to view is obtained it is of the utmost importance that sites, and crops and soils covering or surrounding them, should not be disturbed in any way.

Places to visit

Norwich Castle Museum, Castle Meadow, Norwich
(Norwich 611277)
Yarmouth Museum, 4 South Quay, Great Yarmouth
(Great Yarmouth 855746)
King's Lynn Museum, Old Market Street, King's Lynn
(King's Lynn 5001)
Thetford Ancient House Museum, White Hart Street, Thetford
(Thetford 2599)
Cromer Museum, East Cottages, Tucker Street, Cromer
(Cromer 513543)

Metal detectors

Found objects, other than those of gold and silver, belong to the land and not to the tenant or finder. Gold and silver objects are subject to a Treasure Trove inquest and must be reported to the local Coroner, though this can be done for you by the local museum. It is important to remember that all land belongs to someone, and prior permission to use a metal detector is thus required. Metal detector users are encouraged to report their finds to the Norfolk Museums Service so that objects of interest can be recorded. Sensible use of metal detectors is to be welcomed, and a pamphlet ("Archaeological Finds: Some Suggestions about the Use of Metal Detectors in Norfolk and Suffolk") has been compiled by the Scole Archaeological Committee. Copies are available from the Norfolk Archaeological Unit, Union House, Gressenhall, East Dereham, Norfolk NR20 4DR. In addition a number of special clubs for detector users have been formed. Ask at the Unit for details.

Organisations to join

Norfolk and Norwich Archaeological Society, Garsett House, St.Andrews Hall Plain, Norwich NR3 1AT
Great Yarmouth and District Archaeological Society, c/o Central Library, Great Yarmouth
West Norfolk and King's Lynn Archaeological Society, c/o King's Lynn Museum, King's Lynn
Norfolk Industrial Archaeology Society, c/o the Bridewell Museum, Norwich
Norfolk Archaeological Rescue Group, c/o Norfolk Archaeological Unit, Union House, Gressenhall, East Dereham NR20 4DR
Norfolk Research Committee, c/o 13, Heigham Grove, Norwich.

(A list of other societies is usually available from the Information Service, Norwich Central Library, Bethel Street, Norwich).

The Romano British plough, pulled by a pair of oxen; based on a bronze model found at Piercebridge, in Northumberland.

Index

CELTIC FIRE AND ROMAN RULE

praefectus civitatus 48
Prasutagus (Prasto) 25-29,44,46
procurator 28,47,67
Pye Road 29,56,60

rabbits 75
radishes 75
Red Sea 33
Reedham 82
religion,religious
    12,26,31,44,46,75-79
revolt 23,25,28,43
Rhine 82
Richborough 23
Ricon 25
Ringstead 15,16,32
roads 6,23,55-57,60,80
Roman 9-11,17,19,21-86
Romano British
    20,52,56,59,64,70,74,76-79,88
Rome 23,25-26,36,43,49,79,80,85
rye 63

salt 68
Salthouse 84
Samian 44
samphire 66
Saxon 10,70,82,85
Saxon shore 82-83,86
Scapula,Ostorius 24-26
Scole 56,60,70,71
Scotland,Scots 9,13,29,82
Scythians 33
sea kale 66
Sedgeford 14
Setchey 9
sheep 8,63,68
shield 15,32-34,38,40
ships 47,81
Shouldham 33
signal stations 84
silver 12-15,25,27,44,78,79
slaves 19,35
slings 17
Snettisham 9-10,13-15,25,44,78,79
soldier 24,30,36-39,44,47
South Creake 19
Southwold 10
Spalding 67
Spanish 36
spears 15
spelt 8
spinach 66
St Albans 21,31,40
steel 38
Stiffkey 18,84
Stonea 10,25,67
Stonehenge 11
Stradsett 56
subriprasto 25

Suffolk Archaeological Unit 44
Suffolk 10,22,44,49,71
Sul 76
Swaffham 57
Swanton Morley 24
swords 15,32-34,38,39,40

Tacitus 25-26,28-31,40-41,43
Tas 49,54-55
tax 21,26,43,65,80
temple 22-23,30-31,44,55,76-79
terret rings 35
Thames 19,21,23
Thet 19
Thetford 3,10,17,19,28,44-45,47,78
Thetford Treasure 44,78,79
Thornham 47
Threxton 24,44,56-57,60
Tiberius 22
Tivetshall St Margaret 62
Toftrees 56
Togodumnus 23
torcs 13-15,29
towns 17,19,50-52-53,55-56,80
trade 19
treaty 26
tribunes 39
triclinium 62
Trinovantes 12,19,21,23,30,42
troops 27
turnips 63

Upwell 67

Vandals 85
Venta Icenorum 10,49,50,51
Verulamium 31
vetch 65
villa 60-63

Wales 9,24,26
Warborough Hill 84
Warham 18,47
Warham Camp 17-19
warrior 11,15-17,26-27,
    31,33-35,40-41,48
Water Newton 56
Watling Street 31,40
Watton 56
Waveney 7,56,60,82
Wayford Bridge 56
weapons (see also individual
    weapons) 24,32,34,36
Webster,Dr.Graham 41
Weeting 67
Wells 17
Welsh 70
Wensum 50,81
Wessex 17
West Newton 62